LIFE PURPOSE
BOOT CAMP

ALSO BY ERIC MAISEL

"What a pivotal way to experience your brain and all that it can create! I love that this book celebrates and teaches the concept of productive obsession and the multitudinous gifts of brainstorming."

— SARK, artist and author of *Glad No Matter What* and other books (www.PlanetSARK.com)

Praise for Eric Maisel's Creativity Coaching

"Without Eric Maisel's guidance I would never have successfully negotiated the publishing process. With his help, I completed a substantial proposal, landed a good agent, and just saw my first book published!"

— Nancy Pine, author of *Educating Young Giants*

"It's been an unexpected joy to find someone as creatively supportive and encouraging as Eric Maisel. I didn't know what to expect out of our sessions, and each one is fresh and interesting. Eric is inspirational!"

— Christine Collister, international recording artist

"Eric Maisel's insights have helped me with every aspect of my painting career, from the evolution of my market vision to strategies for self-promotion. I also found his help invaluable in feeding my creator's soul!"

— Jonathan Herbert, painter and photographer

"I began my novel in one of Eric Maisel's Deep Writing workshops, finished it in another, and quickly sold it for a lovely advance. Eric, his individual coaching, and his writing workshops have made all the difference in my writing life."

— Eva Weaver, author of *The Puppet Boy of Warsaw*

"I'm an executive coach and the author of two books, and Eric Maisel is my coach. No one is better qualified to lead a creative person on his or her creative journey."

— Jackee Holder, author of *Be Your Own Best Life Coach*

From Reviews of Eric Maisel's Previous Books

"Eric Maisel's books should be required reading for anyone involved in the arts, especially students and their teachers. Maisel demystifies the process of creating art." — *Theatre Design and Technology*

"Maisel is a meticulous guide who knows the psychological landscape that artists inhabit." — *The Writer* magazine

"Eric Maisel has made a career out of helping artists, musicians, dancers, and writers cope with the traumas and troubles that are the price of admission to a creative life." — *Intuition* magazine

"Eric Maisel has fused his empirical knowledge of the artistic life with true empathy and support for artists in each of the disciplines." — *New Age Journal*

Praise for *Brainstorm* by Eric Maisel and Ann Maisel

"[*Brainstorm*] is a book that should be read by all who want to live their life in a way that is vital and leaves some kind of legacy. It's not about fame and fortune, but rather, about ensuring that this brief span that we have on Earth is one that has value — where we leave some kind of impression. There's nothing that matters more." — *Seattle Post-Intelligencer*

"All too often people overlook the basics of a productive life, distracted by multitasking, marketing, and information overload. With this provocative departure from the usual lifestyle manual, the Maisels are out to break us of those tendencies." — *Publishers Weekly*

"Presents a new way of thinking about how to turn brain potential into passion, energy, and genuine accomplishments." — Camille Minichino, physicist and author of the Periodic Table Mysteries

LIFE PURPOSE BOOT CAMP

The 8-Week Breakthrough Plan for Creating a Meaningful Life

ERIC MAISEL

 New World Library
Novato, California

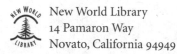

New World Library
14 Pamaron Way
Novato, California 94949

Text design by Tona Pearce Myers

Library of Congress Cataloging-in-Publication Data
Maisel, Eric, date.
 Life purpose boot camp : the 8-week breakthrough plan for creating a meaningful life / Eric Maisel.
    pages   cm
Includes index.
ISBN 978-1-60868-306-2 (paperback)
1. Self-actualization (Psychology) 2. Maturation (Psychology) I. Title.
BF637.S4M334 2014
158.1—dc23   2014018121

First printing, October 2014
ISBN 978-1-60868-306-2
Printed in Canada on 100% postconsumer-waste recycled paper

New World Library is proud to be a Gold Certified Environmentally Responsible Publisher. Publisher certification awarded by Green Press Initiative. www.greenpressinitiative.org

10   9   8   7   6   5   4   3   2   1

For Ann, as always

Contents

INTRODUCTION
Welcome to Life Purpose Boot Camp

Welcome to life purpose boot camp, where you will have the chance to choose your life purposes so that you can experience life as more meaningful. You are about to embark on this eight-week journey — a journey that will change your life.

This endeavor will require real work, hence the metaphor of boot camp. But it is life-changing work. I know you are busy, that you are tired at the end of the day, and that you can't really take on another thing. But this isn't just "another thing." This is a game changer, a life changer, maybe even a lifesaver. I hope you will accept the challenge.

I suspect, since you are holding this book, that you are experiencing some disconnect between the way you are living now and the way you would like to be living. Even if you don't know what your life purposes are, I am guessing that you would like to be more aligned with them. But that is a serious problem, isn't it, not knowing how to name and frame your life purposes? If you're unclear about that pivotal point, how can you aim your life in a more purposeful direction?

At the end of the coming eight weeks, if you choose to enlist in life purpose boot camp, you may experience all the following benefits: you will have named your life purposes, perhaps for the first time; you will have acquired some tools for keeping your life purposes present in your daily life; and you will be living more purposefully, meaningfully, and authentically. So let's get started.

The Metaphor of Boot Camp

As life gets busier and more complex, we all crave something larger and more meaningful than just checking off another item on our to-do lists. Traditionally we've looked to religion and spirituality for a sense of life purpose, but in our secular age the idea of gods or gurus providing this sense of purpose seems less compelling. The need grows stronger every day for new, better answers as traditional answers continue to fall by the wayside.

Certain sorts of secular solutions to this dilemma, such as, "Do what you love" or "Live with passion" sound attractive. But though they possess the virtue of simplicity, they just aren't psychologically sophisticated enough. Human life is complicated, full of stressors and distress, and can't be made to match some fantasy of bliss and ease. Any genuinely fruitful exploration of life purpose has to take human reality into account.

Likewise, such an exploration must get at what meaning really is. You can't construct a meaningful life for yourself if you don't have a clear understanding of the nature of meaning. People flounder as they try to envision their life purpose because they've skipped the necessary step of arriving at a deep personal understanding of this very thing.

Once you understand that meaning is a psychological experience that you can cultivate and create, you suddenly realize three fundamental laws about life purpose: there is no single life purpose for everyone; most people need multiple life purposes; and arriving at an understanding of *your* life purposes requires effort.

You can gain a deep understanding both of your life purposes and of how to achieve them, but you are obliged to work for that understanding, just as you are obliged to work in a real boot camp to learn how to handle, clean, and fire your rifle. Few of our goals in life can be achieved without work. The same is true with respect to choosing our life purposes.

Even though it is human nature to want life to be easy and to hope that unlocking one secret will change everything, we also retain an abiding desire to show up, do the work, and make ourselves proud. Recovery programs prove that; weight-loss programs prove that; military service proves that. Now you can learn to do the necessary work in the area that matters the most to you: living your life purposefully and meaningfully.

With this book I want to help you understand how, by adopting certain ideas and engaging in specific practices, you can effectively meet your pressing life purpose challenges. Today many of us have grave trouble comprehending our life purposes and experiencing life as meaningful. This contemporary problem has clear causes, but here I am more concerned with providing answers than with analyzing the roots of this dilemma.

The headline here is that there *are* answers. Once you understand how meaning operates, how meaning and life purpose are related, and what concrete steps you can take to live as a value-based meaning-maker (an idea I will explain), you will be able to completely transform your life and never run out of meaning again.

But first you must go through boot camp. When I was in the army I first went through basic training and then advanced infantry training. After returning from Asia, I served as a drill sergeant to new recruits. So I have experienced boot camp from both sides. Boot camp is a very interesting place with many metaphoric resonances that we can apply to the idea of life purpose. Here are a few of those resonances.

Radical Lifestyle Change

First, things change immediately when you enter the army. As soon as you arrive at boot camp you are in a completely new environment and governed by entirely different rules. Hardly any event in a person's life produces such a radical change from one day to the next. In the course of this book, you will go from living in an ordinary way one day and deciding to live as a meaning-maker the next. That change is exactly as radical as enlisting, if we let it be!

Continual Testing

Second, you are continually tested in basic training, and it is made clear that you are *being* continually tested. Whether it's the test of a long run with full gear on, the test of dealing with a room full of tear gas as you learn to get your gas mask on, the test of marksmanship as you learn each new weapon, or the physical test that you have to pass to graduate basic training, boot camp is a continual testing ground. So is life. By acknowledging this we stand a little straighter and a little more at the ready to choose our life purposes.

Morning "Falling In"

Third, in boot camp the first thing you do every day is "fall in." That is, you leave your barracks and get into company formation and stand at attention while you are counted and while the day's instructions are announced. The metaphor of falling in very nicely captures what a morning meaning check-in can feel like as you decide daily where to invest meaning. Rather than standing at attention, we start our day *with* attention: we face our day and make mindful decisions. The ceremonial falling in of boot camp mirrors our individual daily falling in as we start our day with intention.

Quick Thinking and Quick Acting

Fourth, in boot camp you're taught to seize opportunities and to act quickly, since your life may depend on it. For example, if you are captured, your best and perhaps only chance to escape is in the first seconds of capture before you are put completely under enemy control. In everyday life most people see no need to live in such a heightened fashion, acting quickly and making every second count. Yet our life purposes may require that we live exactly that way, staying more alert than usual and acting more quickly. You become the quick-witted, quick-acting project manager of the project of your life.

Repetitive Practice

Fifth is the idea of drill. Soldiers are made to march in part for physical conditioning but just as much to instill in them an acceptance of the monotony of military life, a monotony of marching, cleaning weapons, and waiting for something to happen. Life requires that same acceptance of unexciting repetition. To successfully play an instrument you must repetitively practice that instrument. To successfully build a business you must involve yourself in repetitive business activities. To successfully run a scientific experiment you must check on your rats daily. Life possesses a repetitive aspect that we must accept. Indeed, precision drill possesses a certain beauty, and we can take a surprising amount of pride in drilling well, the same kind of pride we can experience when we do a beautiful job at our own repetitive activities.

Regular Inspections

Sixth, we must undergo inspection. In boot camp you are regularly inspected to see if your belt buckle is shining, if your weapon is clean, if your fatigues have been pressed, and so on. While you're being inspected you stand at attention to underscore how seriously you take this inspection. There is a certain lovely gravity to standing up straight and forthrightly dealing with a tarnished belt buckle or wrinkled fatigues. If we are intending to act responsibly, we have to monitor ourselves to make sure that we are doing precisely that — and the word *inspection* nicely captures the flavor of that self-monitoring process.

Tapping Into Our Reserves

Finally, there is the idea of tapping into our reserves. In boot camp a recruit is invited up to the front and told to hold his rifle out at arm's length. Naturally he can only do this for so long. The recruit struggles more and more to keep his rifle up. Finally he can't help but lower it — and it seems indisputable that he has used up every ounce of his strength. At this point the drill sergeant shouts, "Mister, get that rifle up!" and the recruit instantly returns the rifle to the raised position.

The recruit had reserves of strength that he — and everyone watching — had no idea he possessed. We too have reserves we don't know we possess. Of course, we don't want to access these reserves by yelling at ourselves like internal drill sergeants. But we *do* want to know that we possess these reserves and that if one of our life purposes stretches us past our comfort level, we will be able to tap into our reserves to help us along.

You can make it through life doing your work, entering relationships, having a glass of wine, watching the evening news, and putting one foot in front of the other. We are built to be able to make it through life like that, though we are also built to become sad if that is the entirety of our life. We grow sad because we know that by not articulating our life purposes and by not manifesting those purposes, we have fallen short of living authentically.

On the one hand, why not just live, since that is taxing enough? No cosmic arbiter cares if that is all we do, and half the time we don't really care, either. On the other hand, we know that we have an obligation to ourselves to make our time on earth worthy. We wake up each day on the horns of that quintessentially human dilemma: Shall I just go through the motions, which is hard enough, or shall I try to inject some purpose into my day? Most days we settle for the former.

If you would prefer to live a life of purpose regularly and not just sporadically, then I suggest you do three things, all of which we'll discuss in detail in this book: get clear on your life purposes, upgrade your personality, and manage your circumstances as mindfully as you can. If you do these three things, you will make yourself proud.

Some heavy lifting will be involved: the psychological heavy lifting of adopting a new attitude and a new vision of life and the practical heavy lifting of manifesting that attitude and that vision in the real world. That amounts to a lot, but the reward is the highest prize available to you: an authentic life.

Natural Psychology: A Brief Introduction

Over the past several years I've been developing a new sort of psychology that I call "natural psychology," which focuses on our very human need for meaning and life purpose. In this section I want to present you with a pared-down but hopefully clear vision of natural psychology's views with respect to meaning and life purpose.

No life purposes can even exist until you step back and identify, embrace, and implement ones of your own choosing. There is no one meaning of life but rather a multitude of subjective life meanings, and there is no one purpose to life but rather a multitude of subjective life purposes.

Each person must sort out her life purposes and life meanings, realize that she is the arbiter of these purposes and meanings, and proceed to make value-based meaning — meaning that takes into account her values and principles.

There are many ways to garner the psychological experience of meaning. You might have that experience just by gazing up at the night sky. But we make ourselves proudest when we strive for meaning that is rooted in our values and principles. Therefore, we are confronted not only by the task of making meaning but also by the higher, harder task of making *value-based* meaning. In this way we achieve a life at once meaningful *and* principled. Living this way is a *decision*.

We might wish that the situation were otherwise. We might wish that life had a single meaning and a single purpose rather than being this self-determined affair full of multiplicities and contradictions. But the part of us that knows best realizes that we have evolved into exactly the sort of creature who finds himself in exactly these circumstances. There is no universal agenda that, if we were able to discern it, would provide us with guidelines for living and reasons for living.

That is why natural psychology is called "natural," as in naturalistic. It takes as its starting point the reality of evolution and the fact that individuals and species come and go. Species come into existence not because anyone or anything cares about them but because animated life is possible. Once animated life comes into existence, it is predictable in its rhythms and in the challenges it is obliged to face.

What are some of these predictable challenges with respect to life purpose? Consider a few simple examples. Let's say you construe it to be your life purpose to build bridges. However, you find it's impossible to contrive opportunities to build the bridges you want to erect. No one will hire you to build bridges; building small bridges over creeks is not what you had in mind; life refuses to provide you with a meaningful way to build bridges. Your life purpose and the facts of existence seem completely out of alignment. How could this situation produce anything but pain, distress, and a terrible taste in the mouth? The same kind of scenario might pertain to becoming a concert pianist, playing professional basketball, or flying jets. You form a life purpose — and then life doesn't allow it.

Or say that you see your life purposes as getting some satisfaction out of life, living ethically, and doing a little good. At the same time, you deeply want writing poetry to be your life's work. Over time you realize that writing poetry doesn't actually bring you that much satisfaction, that you aren't sure how it amounts to ethical action, and that you can't see how it is doing any real good. In this example your life purposes make complete sense to you, and your feeling for poetry is entirely genuine, and yet those two realities fail to mesh. Which is supposed to give way to the other?

These two simple examples help us to understand why human beings have such trouble with both the concept and the reality of life purpose. On the concept level, we suppose that having a life purpose must amount to a sort of blessing and a blueprint for living. In reality, possessing a life purpose, or multiple life purposes, may amount only to added difficulty. That's why we need life purpose boot camp to help us prepare for — and overcome! — these very real difficulties.

Many people grow up receiving messages about meaning and life purpose that are very different from the ones I'm articulating here and as a result find it difficult to adopt this new way of thinking. Therefore, the bedrock axioms listed below may require some study. I think that if you drill down on them by reading them over a few times, you will gain some important understanding.

You need not agree with all of them to benefit from life purpose boot camp, but I would like you to know where I am coming from in this book. Whether your orientation is secular, as mine is, or spiritual/religious, you are still obliged to name and frame your life purposes and incorporate them into your daily life. Many people with a spiritual orientation have found life purpose boot camp valuable in helping them clarify their life purposes and organize their life around them. I think you too will see how most, if not all, these axioms apply to you:

1. We are evolved creatures, not designed creatures. If we were designed with some life purpose in mind, we would need to know what that purpose was so that we

could live in alignment with it. But the universe provides us with no answers. We are obliged to decide for ourselves not only what our life purposes are but also what we take the phrase *life purpose* to mean.

2. There are no life purposes to seek (as if we were sheep who had lost our way). Instead of seeking, we must *decide*. We must decide whether the phrase even interests us, and, if it does, what it means and implies. To repeat, life purpose is not a given — it's a decision.

3. If you don't decide to *have* life purposes, you will not have them. You may stay very busy, you may experience pleasure and acquire things, but none of that is the same as having life purpose.

4. The following is one way to construe life purpose: a life purpose is a decision to honor something as more important than something else. It is a decision to represent yourself in a certain way because representing yourself in that way makes you feel proud of your efforts. It is a decision to value something, to stand for something, to get something out of life, to give something to life.

5. Naturally, you might construe life purpose in some other way. One of the goals of this book is to help you name and frame for *yourself* what *life purpose* means to you. This can be a painstaking process and may lead you through a maze of false starts, contradictions, and confusions. But the end result is worth it.

6. The terms *life purpose* and *meaning* are fundamentally related. Life purpose is the decision you make. Meaning is a psychological experience. In the sentence

"I want to live a joyful life, but I am not enjoying life today," the first part of the sentence reflects your intention, and the second part reflects your experience. Both intention and experience are important, but intention is more important. You *choose* your life purposes, but you *cross your fingers* for meaningful experiences.

7. Even though you can't guarantee the experience of meaning any more than you can guarantee the experience of joy, you can still be smart about meaning and think through what might provoke that experience. "I am going to try this because it might bring me joy" is an analogous sentence to "I am going to try this because it may prove meaningful." We call this "thing you might try" a meaning opportunity.

8. Say that one of your life purposes is to "understand the human condition." To that end, you might seize the meaning opportunity of getting a graduate degree in social sciences. Naturally you can't know if the program you enroll in or your subsequent career will prove meaningful or will serve this particular life purpose. You still have to monitor its progress. A meaning opportunity is something you try: it is a guess, an adventure, a hope, a calculation. Whether or not it pans out remains to be seen.

9. You can be living your life purposes even if on a given day you are not experiencing life as meaningful. This is crucial to remember. Since meaning is merely a certain sort of psychological experience, like any psychological experience it comes and goes. Maybe

the nonfiction book you're writing is stumping you and you are dismayed and disappointed. If one of your life purposes is to tell truth to power and that is what you are attempting in the book, you can remind yourself that you are living your life purposes, even though you aren't experiencing today's writing as meaningful. Or maybe the three graduate classes you're taking are all boring. They haven't panned out as meaning opportunities but you are still living your life purpose. Your life purposes are independent of and different from your experience of meaning.

10. Both your intentions (your life purposes) and your experiences (your experience of meaningfulness) are important. Therefore, you want to keep them both in mind. One way to hold both these ideas at the same time is to focus on being a "value-based meaning-maker." In this phrase, the "value-based" part signals that you have values, principles, and life purposes that you intend to manifest. The "meaning-maker" part signals that you are taking responsibility for making meaning and living your life purposes by "making meaning investments" and "seizing meaning opportunities." This phrase can do a lovely job of holding everything you need to know about both life purpose and meaning.

11. Just because you've named and framed your life purposes doesn't mean that you are equal to living them. You can name a life purpose that still may be out of your reach because you're drinking alcoholically, overly anxious, trapped in debilitating circumstances, and so on. It naturally follows that entering

recovery, reducing your anxiety, and changing your circumstances must be added to your life purposes. If your life purpose is x and it has a prerequisite of y, then y must also become one of your life purposes. Because these are such important elements of the process, in boot camp we will spend a week on each: a week on upgrading your personality and a week on dealing with your circumstances.

12. The language I'm employing, which includes phrases such as *value-based meaning-making, meaning investments, meaning opportunities, available personality,* and *personality upgrade,* will help you navigate this territory. Many people are put off by this language and find it too abstract and too difficult. Others use it as an opportunity to skip boot camp. I ask you to bear with me and give this language a try. It just might make an important difference in your life.

On the Bridge

To drive the point home a bit further, I'd like to share a story as an example of just how dark and difficult life can get if we don't get meaning and life purpose right — and how much better life can be if we do. Bill, a successful accountant, wrote me the following:

Dr. Maisel,

I am in debt to you, since you have provided me with a framework that I have been searching for for many years now. Your work has transformed my life, and I am feeling healthier than I have in a very long time.

I was on a bridge in August 2012, convinced that the only logical thing for me to do was to jump, since life is a cosmic joke. It sounded crazy to people who knew me. I had a beautiful wife of twenty-two years, three grade-school kids, and an MBA, and I was an experienced sales professional. But the pain that I was experiencing as I left a Christian worldview and tried to embrace...well, that was the point. I didn't know what to embrace. All I knew was that for years I had been wrestling with whether or not I was an atheist, and when I finally admitted to myself that I was, my world was turned into complete chaos.

A dear childhood friend talked me down off the bridge via text messaging and rushed me to a hospital, where he would not allow me to leave unless I agreed to be treated. Thus I got an up-close view of what passes for help from mental-health experts! I checked myself out after my second group session, where I witnessed the psychologist browbeating and berating a confused young woman and using baited questions to drive her to his preformed conclusion about her problems.

Now, a full thirteen months later, after having read your ideas about natural psychology and implementing them, I am doing great! In fact, my wife said to me this morning, "This has been one of the best weeks of our marriage." Can you believe that? That after twenty-two years together, and after I put her through hell, things have turned around that much? It wasn't easy, but I feel very fortunate that I found your work. Both your views and the language you've created make sense to me and give me a way to live with new purpose and passion.

I know my friends are a little skeptical. I'm following the teachings of a guy who has a new "psychology thing," and I'm feeling "great," and self-reporting that my wife thinks I'm a new man! But to my skeptical friends I can only say, "Why not?" They all know my bent against cults and shams and my desire to keep asking questions and seeking truth. My reading, research, and contemplation have left me feeling comfortable enough to say I'm not being hoodwinked. Natural psychology is really working for me. I am a new man.

I feel alive and I have hope again. I'm not afraid to do the self-work that I need to continue to do to be the father, husband, and friend I desire to be. Even my job has turned around, and that has given me a much-needed confidence boost to get back to employing my talents and playing to my strengths. So I am telling my friends that if they know of anyone wired like me who may be having an existential crisis or who can't seem to shake their depression, they should feel free to point them my way. Then I can share my experience with them and hope they find a path to healing and hope like I did.

Thank you,
Bill

Using This Book

Before we dive in, let me briefly explain the book's organizational scheme. In weeks 1 and 2 we begin with meaning, because we need to know what provokes the psychological experience of meaning and what it feels like when we pay attention to meaning. This knowledge helps us make smarter life purpose decisions. Because we also need to consider our personality and our circumstances in order to live our life purposes, these are the subjects of weeks 3 and 4. Then we are ready to move on to the work of naming, framing, and living our life purposes, the work of weeks 5 through 8. Your work on meaning, personality, and circumstance is an important prerequisite to your work on life purpose!

Each week's lesson comes with questions to answer. To really participate in boot camp, you will need to take the time to answer the questions and to write out your answers. Otherwise, you'll just be reading a book. That reading may help you, even dramatically, but there is no substitute for doing the work. You can read about how to disassemble and reassemble a rifle, or you can disassemble one and reassemble it yourself.

Let's begin! I salute you for embarking on this adventure.

Creating Your Menu
of Meaning Opportunities

I'd like you to begin your boot camp adventure by thinking deeply about what I'm calling "meaning opportunities." Let me repeat a few headlines before we launch into a close examination. The first headline is that meaning is a psychological experience that you might experience accidentally (as when you look up at the night sky) or that you can create through your conscious efforts to experience it.

Naturally you want and need that experience: all human beings do. But more important than the experience of meaning is the decision to live *your* way, that is, to live according to your life purposes. Once you understand that it is more important to manifest your values, principles, intentions, and life purposes than it is to experience meaning, you arrive at the wonderful — and calming — understanding that you do not have to look for meaning, wait for meaning, fight for meaning, or miss meaning. All you have to do is live your intentions and be human.

That isn't to say that experiencing meaning is trivial. Of course it isn't. If you go too long without it, say, because you've chosen a profession that isn't providing you with the experience of meaning, you must do something about it. Meaning isn't irrelevant. So it is good to know when you actually experience it. Most people have very little idea about which activities, actions, or states of being actually provoke this psychological experience. Do you?

If asked, people are likely to give a reflexive answer such as "being out in nature" or "spending time with my loved ones" or "creating something in my studio." These may indeed be among their meaning opportunities but others, small and large, abound. People are unlikely to consider how meaning-ful it feels to them to play with their cat, take their kid out for ice cream, stay calm in a situation that usually makes them anxious, walk down a busy city street taking in the sights, see a good movie, or stand up to injustice. Most people have not given much thought or even any thought to *all* the meaning opportunities in their life.

Why the Language You Use Matters

Many folks also have given little or no thought to the lan-guage they use to discuss meaning with themselves. People typically get stymied trying to answer the question, "What would it be meaningful to do next?" because it is the wrong question to ask. Embedded in that question is the idea that the experience of meaning can be guaranteed. The logic of such a sentence is, "Certain things are meaningful, so let me choose one and get me some meaning."

But nothing is *necessarily* meaningful. Playing with your infant child might feel tremendously meaningful one day and more like a chore the next day. Working on your novel might feel poignantly meaningful today and completely pointless tomorrow. Your teaching job might feel meaningful during your first five years of teaching and empty and burdensome in your twentieth. "What would it be meaningful to do?" has an implicit guarantee built into it that life can't possibly meet.

That's why in natural psychology we use two phrases, *meaning opportunities* and *meaning investments*, to help avoid even a whiff of that guarantee. We paint a different picture of meaning. Meaning is something we can aim for and try to create by investing our time, energy, and human resources in a given effort, activity, initiative, or way of being. It is also something that we can wish for by seizing some meaning opportunity, crossing our fingers, and hoping for the best. By making meaning investments and by seizing meaning opportunities we actively organize our day around making meaning.

To get to this evolved understanding, that you can hope for meaning and try to make meaning but not *guarantee* meaning, you may have to change your beliefs, move to a place of acceptance and surrender about the human condition, and heal a lot of regret that it has taken you so long to reach this understanding. There will still be necessary elaborations, refinements, and steps to take. But that is a wonderful starting place: arriving at the understanding that meaning is a psychological experience, that it comes and goes, that it is less important than your life purposes and your values and principles, and that you can organize your day around making meaning investments, seizing meaning opportunities, and engaging in value-based meaning-making.

Let me repeat this point to underscore it. Why not use the phrase *do something meaningful* instead of the more awkward-sounding *seize meaning opportunities*, *make meaning investments*, and *make value-based meaning*? Isn't *do something meaningful* a more natural, straightforward way to say the same thing? Actually, it isn't. That phrase has embedded in it the idea that a prospective choice is already known to be meaningful and will prove to be meaningful. But we can't know that.

To pretend we can know that choosing anthropology or engineering as our life work will feel consistently meaningful, that choosing this man or this woman as our mate will feel consistently meaningful, that choosing this value over that value or this principle over that principle will feel consistently meaningful is to set ourselves up for existential pain. We can't know such things, any more than we can know that something we intend to try will always prove awesome or joyful. *Psychological experiences are not guaranteed*. To imagine that they can be is to be on the wrong footing with life.

Consider some analogies. When a person says, "Let me do something joyful," she expects that thing to feel joyful. When a person says, "Let me do something calming," she expects that thing to calm her. When a person says, "Let me do something exciting," she expects that thing to prove exciting. In these cases, the individual is disappointed if she doesn't experience joy, if she isn't calmed, or if she doesn't have an exciting time. She feels she has wasted her time. Worse yet, she can be thrown into doubt about whether she even knows what things produce joy, calmness, or excitement. The absence of the hoped-for experience produces a small crisis.

This becomes a big crisis if you are hoping for the experience of meaning. It is a big crisis if you spend two years writing a novel, three years in a training program, or five years in a doctoral program and do not experience meaning either as you proceed or, worse yet, as you finish. Throughout you can say to yourself, "Okay, this doesn't feel meaningful now but it will in the end" and soothe yourself a little. But at the end, now that you have a finished novel, a certificate, or a degree and you *still* aren't experiencing meaning, now, *that* is a genuine crisis.

Let's look at this matter the other way around. Say that you are contemplating working on your novel, making travel arrangements to attend a protest march, preparing to mind your colicky grandchild, looking for funding for your start-up business, or planning not to drink alcohol for a month. You know for certain that the thing you are contemplating is not going to feel particularly meaningful and may amount to something between slogging hard work and full-out frustration. If you know this in your heart, how can you say, "This is going to prove meaningful"? But you *can* say, "As a value-based meaning-maker I am doing this because it aligns with my values, principles, and life purposes; I intend to make a real investment in doing this; and maybe, just maybe, it will ultimately prove to be a meaning opportunity." The latter takes longer to say but is ever so much wiser!

Creating Your Menu

Anything can be a meaning opportunity because anything can provoke the psychological experience of meaning. You might get out of your chair, go to the window, look out at the sky, and experience meaning. In this scenario it was opportune of you to walk to the window and look out. Maybe you suspected you would experience meaning, because looking at the sky regularly provokes that feeling in you. Maybe you had a hunch that it was time to get up and look out the window. Walking to the window and looking out was an intentional act.

Or maybe you got up and moved to the window unconsciously, looked out, smiled to yourself, returned to your chair, and hardly registered that you just experienced a meaningful moment. Whether the act of walking to the window and looking out at the sky occurred consciously or unconsciously, whether it registered as a meaningful moment or not, it was opportune that you did it. That action earned you some meaning.

You arrived at the window and had a meaningful experience. The same is potentially true about anything we might name: it might be opportune to play with your cat, to move halfway around the world, to donate to your favorite charity, to smile, to call your sister, to sweat bullets for the sake of your new business. Anything, small or large, might prove opportune and provoke the psychological experience of meaning. Anything, including surprising things, scary things, and unpleasant things, may prove a meaning opportunity.

Yet although anything might provoke the experience of meaning, many things *stand out* as meaning opportunities. People regularly experience each of the following as a meaning opportunity: love and relationships; service and stewardship; good works and ethical action; excellence, achievement, and a good career; experimentation, excitement, and adventure; creativity and self-actualization; sensory stimulation and pleasure; and states of being such as contentment and appreciation. This is not an exhaustive list, but it is a suggestive list — it suggests the intimate relationship between value and meaning; it suggests how "doing" can provoke the experience of meaning but how "being" can also provoke it; and it begins to paint a picture of how a life can be knitted together around meaning opportunities.

How you talk to yourself about your meaning opportunities will naturally be personal and idiosyncratic. Here is how one internal conversation might go: "My big sources of meaning are my work and the people I love. But I know that keeping to a certain disciplined regimen, in which I exercise, eat well, and create is a big help to me in keeping meaning afloat. Therefore I am putting exercise and meal preparation into the category of meaning opportunities rather than into the category of chores. I'm likewise putting creating into that same category, even though I have doubts about whether what I paint is any good. My hope is that if I pay attention to the big meaning investments I've made in my work and in the people I love, and if I also seize daily meaning opportunities like exercising and creating, I will experience life as meaningful."

By keeping your eye on the main point, that while the experience of meaning can't be guaranteed you can still aim yourself in its direction and make reasoned efforts to experience it, you become relatively free from *needing* any of your efforts to produce that experience. You have positioned yourself to create more meaning. You learn how to take risks in the service of meaning, just as you take a risk when you invest in the stock market, a certain career, a certain creative effort, a certain relationship, a certain adventure, or a certain conversation. You keep your eyes peeled for your next meaning opportunities, you make short-range plans and long-range plans for seizing such opportunities, you live your life purposes, and you assess your experiences. In this way you stay on top of meaning.

You must regularly monitor your experiences because you may not have gotten lucky, some major meaning investment may not be paying off, and you may have to make some big changes. Say that you opt for stewardship; choose a career in environmental protection; achieve some successes, some near successes, and many failures; and discover that you are not being gifted with the experience of meaning from your efforts. You may still hold stewardship as one of your life purposes, but you must reckon with the reality that you are receiving too little meaning from your environmental efforts. These crises and conflicts arise all the time in the lives of real people, and when they arise they *require our attention*.

What elementary school teacher, novelist, environmentalist, actor, attorney — what human being — hasn't found herself at such a crossroads? Who hasn't found himself at such a crossroads in a long-term relationship? Many meaning opportunities and meaning investments will not pan out, even though they completely align with your life purposes. Knowing this, you need not feel shocked or even surprised when such a dreadful thing happens. You do not have to doubt your methods or fret that you have no recourse. In fact, you have clear and ample recourse: to reconsider your life purposes in the light of your actual experiences and see what new meaning opportunities you might seize that align with your reconsidered life purposes.

You can make potent meaning even on days when you aren't rewarded with the experience of meaning. Because you've lived that day in accordance with your values and your life purposes and in alignment with your ideas about meaning, you know that the day was rich in meaning no matter how meaningless it actually felt. *You tried* and that effort carries its own positive valence and, very likely, its own felt sense of meaning. And on many days and for many moments you *will* experience meaning. Because you have these new methods, new language, and a new outlook, the likelihood is great that you will experience enough meaning to be able to say, "Life is meaningful *enough. And* I am living my life purposes!"

Your Work for the Week

This week I'd like you to focus on three activities.

First, create your menu of meaning opportunities. Think through what sorts of activities or ways of being provoke the psychological experience of meaning. Your list might include big, abstract categories such as creating, relationships, service, activism, or "just being," and very specific activities, events, and states of being such as "visiting with Aunt Rose," "looking at some Van Goghs and Gauguins," "practicing loving-kindness," or "spending two hours daily working on my novel." I think you will genuinely enjoy creating this list, but whether you find the task enjoyable or just more work, please do create it. Creating this list is the first step in naming and framing your life purposes.

Second, think through what it would be like to intentionally create a day that included items from your menu of meaning opportunities and that also included the other things that you need to do (like chores and work for pay) and want to do (like watching a television show). What would such a day concretely look like? How might one day differ from another, depending on which meaning opportunities you chose and which tasks and pleasures you included?

Take some time to draw up various schedules or pictures of different days, playing with the notion that a day, to be lived mindfully and intentionally, is really a certain sort of negotiation, a balance of chores, relaxations, and meaning-making efforts. At the beginning of each day, you might want to include a morning meaning check-in, a minute or two that you spend choosing your meaning investments for that day.

Third, pick one of the days you've created, and live it. You might want to live one such day on Tuesday, a different one on Wednesday, a different one on Thursday, and so on, to get a sense of how different days feel. Experiment! This is your work (and maybe your fun) for the week.

At the end of the week, please answer the following questions:

1. How was the "total experience" for you? What transpired, and what did you learn?
2. How hard or easy was it to create a menu of meaning opportunities? Were you surprised by any of the items on your list?
3. How hard or easy was it to create a day that included both regular things (like chores and relaxation) and meaning opportunities?
4. How hard or easy was it to live a day that included both regular things (like chores and relaxation) and meaning opportunities?
5. Did anything else about this process intrigue you?

Okay! Please begin your work.

Olivia: My Excruciatingly Long-Lived Mind-Set

What follow are two reports from participants in my online life purpose boot camp about their first week. Olivia, a web and media producer living in Southern California, described her evolving understanding of meaning:

> It's in my nature not to follow through on things like this boot camp, and on anything that I sense will help me grow or learn something important. I procrastinate and then mourn the loss of opportunity. However, I have felt a huge connection with your ideas. So I knew I could *not* put this one off and decided that I must do everything possible to make time for it and to work as hard as I can against the instinctual urge to avoid dealing with

difficult ideas. I am challenging myself to get the most possible return from this experience.

Whenever I've thought about life purpose, it's always meant following a higher calling to me. I was sent to a religiously affiliated private school through the sixth grade, although I'm not religiously observant now. I often feel guilty about my adult lack of religious faith, and because I have never known what purpose I might have or what purpose God might have for me, I have experienced painful existential crises at various points in my life.

I am now in midlife and in the past four to five years have suffered what you describe as, and what I recently have realized must be, several large "meaning crises": the sudden end of my marriage, big career issues, downsizing my home, illness, and more. But by encountering the boot camp materials I feel hopeful that it might be possible to learn skills and behaviors that can change my thought patterns, my tendencies toward depression, and my persistent feeling of being stuck.

How hard was it to create my menu of meaning opportunities? It seemed like it would be easy. I immediately thought of some specific things, such as viewing artworks or observing the ocean, but I kept putting off making the list. I felt the need to read more about your ideas and delayed brainstorming ideas that were about *me*. Once I got started, I thought of several ideas, but I have a lot more to learn and many more opportunities to add to my list as I remember what is really important to me and as I attune myself to the idea of meaning opportunities.

I instantly recognized that I have often sought pleasurable experiences to try to fill some void in my life, that this was essentially a search for meaning, and that these experiences were not always good for me. I was also surprised to recognize that feelings of great achievement, like graduating from college or receiving praise, stood out for me because they gave me a sense of meaning. I had never looked at them that way before, and there are sadly too few of them. I began to see that pleasure is not a great meaning opportunity for me but that achievement or excellence likely is. This was eye-opening!

The biggest surprise about this whole exercise is the idea that I can bring these meaning opportunities into my life, that I can even make plans to schedule them, instead of waiting and hoping for them to randomly occur. It was a revelation not only that I could create and choose from a list of opportunities but also that I could plan a real day around them. And I loved that these needed to be planned into a day that also necessitated other activities: that I didn't need to quit my job or win the Lotto or ignore my other obligations.

I was also surprised to learn that leisure or recreation could still be thought of as necessary and that it was perfectly okay to have parts of my day that were "meaning neutral." Previously I have always felt guilty about leisure activities. Now, with your help, I realize that reading a good book or watching a good movie is also a major meaning opportunity for me, and that makes it even more okay to give myself permission to make them happen.

So I was able to create and plan several such meaningful days. I am excited by the idea and even think it would be great to schedule a "full meaning day" once a month, a day mostly free of obligations and necessary activities but given over to meaning: visiting a museum, taking a long walk on the beach, and maybe doing an art-movie marathon.

But I have not been able to actually *live a day* like this yet. I hope to do that this week, and I also hope that my habit of wanting to do everything perfectly (my all-or-nothing mentality) will not discourage me from trying this, even if it means inserting very small opportunities into my day to start, or having only one to two days a week when I am successful as I get started.

I am also setting a goal to establish a "being practice" into my morning at least a few times a week, and also just being more aware of every moment passing and how I am in control of my reactions and my ability to add meaning opportunities into each day and moment.

Since all these ideas are so radically different from my current (and excruciatingly long-lived but hopefully soon-to-be-past) mind-set, I know that I will set myself up for failure if I expect each day to be a perfect balance of meaning opportunities and needed activities. Yet I am also wowed and inspired by the way this mind shift could affect my entire outlook.

For example, things I previously believed I should be doing because they were good for me, like exercise or meditation, can actually give me a much-needed meaning opportunity. And that is much more inspiring and motivating than the mere thought that I should be doing them.

Tom: Am I Having Problems with ADD, Depression, Sleep…or Meaning?

Tom, a mixed-media artist living in a small town near San Francisco, shared his experience of listing his meaning opportunities:

I've done all the exercises this week and have been working through the questions at the end of the lesson. I learned how unconscious my meaning experiences have been — and, not surprisingly, to what degree my meaning experiences have been unbidden. That is, I have not consciously sought to create meaning experiences but mostly have experienced them as a happy accident beyond my control.

When I created my list of meaning opportunities, I was surprised to see how many of them were not part of my day-to-day life and weren't even replicable on a daily basis. For instance, one of my meaning experiences is having Sunday breakfast with my wife. Obviously, that's not possible on a Tuesday afternoon. Another was walking in a big city, whether it's San Francisco or some foreign place. Again, obviously, I can't replicate that daily since I don't live in a city. So the questions I'm dealing with now are: What is meaningful about those experiences, and is there something about them that I can transfer to my daily life?

Equally revealing to me was a hard look at the activities that compose my daily routine. I found that *none* of them were meaningful to me. So in order to create sample schedules of meaning-filled days, I need to venture into new activities that I think will create meaning opportunities, and I am using my list of meaning opportunities as a starting point to create them. I am brainstorming on this now.

As to how hard or easy it was to create a day that included both regular things (like chores and relaxation) and meaning opportunities: it was very difficult. But I need to work through this. Yesterday, I tried changing up my routine, all the while reciting the mantra to be conscious of meaning. But that proved not to be enough. Without the structure of a preset schedule, a clearly identified meaning-oriented activity, and a sense of time, I found myself drifting back into habitual behavior — along with the expected anxiety that always ensues when I live aimlessly. And that led to the habitual distractions and diversions that I use to ease my anxiety, behaviors that some would call addictive or compulsive but that I now think of as normal — if not desirable — reactions to constant anxiety.

How hard or easy was it to live a day that included both regular things (like chores and relaxation) and meaning opportunities? I haven't done that yet. But I'm finding that there's a lot of insight to be gleaned from going through these exercises, and that viewing my life through the lens of meaning-making is very revealing.

In the past I've worked with therapists and coaches who've labeled the problem this way and that. One blamed depression and wanted to do endless talk therapy. Another blamed ADD and wanted me on a regimen of drugs. Sleep issues were blamed, and I spent a year with a CPAP machine that I probably didn't need. Viewing my life through a meaning-making lens actually resonates with me; I feel like this might be getting to the heart of the problem.

It is time to engage with your week 1 work and to answer your week 1 questions. If you are reading this midweek, if you have certain special duties or obligations this week, if, in short, you have to figure out how to incorporate this work into your real life, then please do so!

WEEK 2

Creating Your Mix
of Meaning Opportunities

We have been working our way toward a discussion of life purpose by examining meaning first. Our formulation here is that life purpose is more important than meaning: we want to live our life purposes whether or not a given effort provokes the experience of meaning. But we're beginning by trying to understand what *does* provoke that feeling and what meaning investments and meaning opportunities make sense for us. We continue that work this week.

The boot camp model has two ideas embedded in it: repetition and novelty. Repetitive activities such as drilling and weapons practice help you improve. At the same time you learn a new thing or two: hand-to-hand combat, a new weapon, escape tactics. We are using the same model. I'd like you to keep working on what you have learned about organizing your day around your meaning opportunities and your meaning investments even as we push on to some new learning. This means that each week you have two kinds of homework: continuing your work on past lessons and engaging with new material.

Let's continue.

What Gets in the Way of Value-Based Meaning-Making?

Your goal, if you would like to live authentically and in alignment with your life purposes, is to make sufficient meaning *and* to have that meaning arise from and support your values.

A sunny day, a bit of tomfoolery: anything might provoke the experience of meaning. That unbidden meaning is of secondary importance to the meaning that you make *your* way, in line with your values and life purposes. You take the phrase *making meaning* to stand for your thoughtful judgments about *how* you want to provoke the psychological experience of meaning and not as an imperative to provoke those experiences at any cost.

Ah, but the effort to make value-based meaning is such a serious and challenging one! It is not at all simple or straightforward to do the right thing when you want to do the impulsive thing. It is ever so hard to honor your values when your liberty or your ease is at stake. It is tremendously challenging to escape from or transcend your formed personality, with its habitual demands and its repetitive thoughts. It is quite a project even to know *what* values to support in the real-life situations that tumble before us one after another.

The phrase *value-based meaning-making* is simple, beautiful, and powerful and also very hard to live up to. Nature, without concern for the consequences of its processes, has produced a creature that can picture righteous living but, because of its exact endowment, can't manage it all that regularly. What we *can* do is begin to identify some of the common obstacles that stand in the way of our value-based meaning-making efforts. Here are ten of them. As troublesome as the first seven challenges may prove, the last three are even more troubling.

Turning a Blind Eye on Value

One obstacle is the way we can turn a blind eye on value. It is both common and easy, for instance, to make a large investment in something that serves us — something that serves our ego needs, our safety needs, or our financial needs — but that is actually morally repugnant to us. That expedient choice becomes the elephant in the room, and we organize our inner life around not noticing our unethical choice.

Consider a person who prides himself on his "values" but can't walk away from his high-paying job as a tobacco executive, even though he knows all about the health risks associated with smoking cigarettes. Since he is not reporting any psychological difficulties and he is a hardworking, upstanding member of his community, current psychology might look at him not only as normal but even as a paragon of normalcy. Yet doesn't he know somewhere inside that he is living unethically?

His community may well make him man of the year for his charitable efforts. He himself may be almost completely defended against admitting that his job kills people. Nevertheless, he most likely retains at least a partial awareness of the elephant in his room. For the sake of his comfort, his prestige, and his paycheck and for other powerful reasons, he has failed to make value-based meaning in this one area — and that one failure may amount to an internal indictment of his whole life. It is easy to picture the whole edifice of his life crumbling when, say, his wife is diagnosed with lung cancer.

Many people who intend to do the right thing often find themselves supporting choices that they do not value or that they even actively detest. Career soldiers who value patriotism and find themselves fighting in a war they hate, career police officers who find themselves paired with a corrupt partner but who can't see breaking the code of silence, career academics who have stopped believing in the worth of their subject matter: each may be plagued by an elephant in their room. Their value-based meaning-making efforts are thwarted and mocked by some large shadow in the center of their life.

Giving In to Desires

A second enormous challenge is the way that desires affect us and the way we are pulled to give in to those desires. We may crave drugs, we may chase a dream that excites us despite its shady values, we may let sexual arousal turn our life upside down and watch the ethical life we have built for ourselves be torn asunder by one guilty orgasm. All that is human and happens regularly.

At such times those desires may even feel meaningful. As we are sitting across from an attractive person who is not our partner and feeling wanted and excited, relishing the archetypal power of that fairy-tale moment, it is easy enough to be suffused not only with desire but also with the sense that nothing could feel more meaningful than this. We are built to have these exact feelings and to make these exact mistakes.

Not Knowing Which Values to Uphold

Third, you may well not know which of your values to uphold in a given situation. It is one thing to value compassion, discipline, freedom, and gratitude. Those are four fine, laudable values. But what will you do when the principal at the school where you teach begins to censor your class materials? Feel gratitude that you still have your job and that your principal didn't do worse and, because you are feeling grateful, ignore his intrusions? Feel compassion for his concerns and the pressures on him to prevent free expression and take his side by not speaking out? Decide to continue acting in a disciplined fashion as a teacher — decide, that is, that the way through this moment is by maintaining a disciplined attitude? Or fight for freedom by speaking up and taking action? Any one of these decisions might be value based and might align with one of your values — but how different the reactions are!

To take a second example along these lines, say that you identify yourself as a spiritual person, engage in practices that you consider spiritual, and hold a view of the universe that includes ideas like "universal mind" and "spiritual oneness." You know that you want your efforts at making meaning to be informed by your understanding of the nature of the universe, but you feel stuck translating ideas like universal mind and spiritual oneness into nameable values. Then a situation arises — say, a diagnosis of a life-threatening illness.

Now you find yourself doubly stuck, torn between taking an active Western-medicine stand and "trusting the universe" to provide healing. Part of this painful conflict has to do with your not really knowing how to apply your beliefs in the context of treating a life-threatening illness. Do your beliefs suggest and even demand a certain sort of passivity? Are you obliged not only to supplement your medical practices with spiritual healing but also to go a giant step further and *substitute* those practices? You know that you want to make meaning, especially now as you confront your illness, but you aren't sure how to make meaning or even how to construe your own values.

Rationalization

Fourth, we can defensively turn a desire into a value through rationalization or some other defense mechanism. Take the preceding example of the teacher and his principal. Say that the teacher opts for compassion, a perfectly laudable value, and keeps silent about the censorship, arguing internally that his principal is under a lot of pressure and that the compassionate action is to support him at this difficult moment. Perhaps this is the teacher manifesting a value and making value-based meaning, and perhaps it isn't.

He may in fact know in a corner of his consciousness that he is not really practicing compassion but rather protecting his job and his current way of life. Or he may really not know that he has made this defensive decision and argue long and loud that he is doing the ethical thing. It is a feature of our species that, because we want to seem ethical to ourselves, we will call an action ethical even when we've chosen it for some other, more shadowy reason. This happens all the time.

Wild-Goose Chasing Values

Fifth, you may "wild-goose chase" values. You might, for example, want to pay your rent, be a responsible person, help send your children to college. Yet for many pressing reasons — because gambling excites you, because you know that you don't earn enough money to actually meet your obligations, and because it is mind-numbing work to keep your life afloat — you spend a great deal of your paycheck on lottery tickets. This hopeful, hopeless gesture is your version of a wild-goose chase: you argue that you are doing a reasonable thing and maybe even the only plausible thing in your situation, but the values that you claim to be supporting — like paying the rent or sending your children to college — are not actually being served.

Competing Aims

The sixth challenge occurs when we have competing aims — and we have them all the time — and one or another of those aims announces itself so loudly that it drowns out our voice of reason. It is one of nature's cruel jokes that it turns up the volume to high when it wants us to notice something. To use the analogy of needing to relieve yourself, in the beginning your need is only mild and you can manage to ignore it. If you ignore it too long, however, your body will announce very loudly that you have waited a long time to find a bathroom. At that moment nothing feels more important.

Likewise we start shouting at ourselves that we desperately need that Scotch, that our team must win or else we'll die, that those shoes are just so beautiful and damn the cost, that life is pathetic and a complete fraud, that this town is so boring that we must get away — we don't just think those thoughts, we *shout* them at ourselves and won't let up. At that moment nothing feels more important than whatever we are shouting about. How easy is it to make value-based meaning while your being is shouting at you about this, that, and the other thing?

Shifting Values

A seventh challenge, one of the more poignant ones, is that our values shift. One day you may value beauty and decide that writing poetry amounts to making value-based meaning. A year later you may decide that poetry is mere words and that you value action rather more. Two years later, having worked a lot in the world, you may find yourself flooded by the feeling that poetry possesses far more value and produces more meaning than the work you've been doing. The value of poetry may shift countless times as you live your life. Each shift amounts to a small earthquake and a real meaning crisis.

Irrationality

Who knows: we may simply not be rational enough for authentic living. Who can say whether our species actually tips the scales on the side of reason? Aristotle observed that as soon as you choose a word like *rational* to describe our species, you've falsified the picture. We are not rational *or* irrational, good *or* evil, but rather exactly who and what we are, enslaved by the words we use to describe ourselves as well as inadequately described by those words. Maybe this creature that we are is so split in devilishly disparate ways, so evolutionarily constructed out of primitive ooze and high ideals, that it can chatter all day long about meaning but still not be able to do anything about its nightmares, its envies, or its fantasies.

It is pleasant to think that we are essentially reasonable — but are we, really? Is anyone really evolved enough or serious enough to make meaning? And can even the small minority of smart, serious prospective meaning-makers really rise to the occasion; deal with their phantoms, desires, and the problems of living; and opt for a life in which they make value-based meaning? The jury is still out on that question.

Insufficient Motivation

Ninth, just as we may not be rational enough for this enterprise, we may not be motivated enough for it. As much as we care about our values, principles, and life purposes, maybe we *don't* care even more. Maybe we are essentially as indifferent about our fate as the universe is about its and ours. In that sense, maybe we are perfect little replicas of the universe. Meaning is infinite; indifference is infinite. Which is the truer statement?

The Rush of Time

Tenth and last — last for our discussion, that is, not the last of the challenges faced by a prospective value-based meaning-maker — is the very nature of "now." Now passes instantly.

There it went again. Soon a minute will have passed, an hour, a day. The rapid passage of time is a complete antimeaning machine. Doesn't life absolutely require tactical slowing down if a person, even a smart, serious, concerned one, is to find the time and space to make meaning? As it stands, the rush of time can rush meaning right off the table.

This is the hand we have been dealt. If we can make value-based meaning *despite all this*, we certainly deserve a round of applause.

In case you would like to think about these ten challenges for a moment longer, following are the ten challenges reframed as questions that you might pose to, and answer, yourself.

1. Is some large ethical dilemma in my life (like that of the tobacco executive) making it hard for me to reach my goal of making value-based meaning?
2. Are my desires so at war with my values that they regularly trump my ability to make value-based meaning?
3. Am I clear on how to choose values in the moment, when many values compete for my attention?
4. Do I regularly turn desires into values through rationalization?
5. Do I "wild-goose chase" value by doing things that I claim support my life purposes but that really don't?
6. Am I in the habit of shouting so loudly about pressing matters that I can't hear myself think about value?
7. Do I know how to handle the painful reality of values shifting?

8. Am I a member of a species equal to making value-based meaning?
9. Am I motivated enough, and do I care enough, to live my life purposes?
10. Do I experience "now" as passing by so quickly that I can't seem to focus on meaning or value?

Your Work for the Week

The preceding discussion should have helped make it a little clearer why creating a menu of meaning opportunities and trying to implement that menu daily isn't quite enough. More thought and more tactics are required. Here is your next tactic: creating a personal mix of meaning opportunities that allows you to experience life as meaningful.

If you think about all the possible foods in the world, you will discover that you are standing in a different relationship to each food item. You may, for example, respect but not love peas and love but not respect ice cream and both love and respect bread. This doesn't make a serving of peas, a scoop of ice cream, or a slice of bread better or worse than the other. But it does mean that you are in a different relationship with each one and that to keep all three on your menu requires a certain kind of awareness and effort.

It will be easy to keep the peas off your plate if you only respect them and neither love nor crave them. It will be hard not to consume too much bread if you both love it and respect it and maybe even crave it. What's the short answer to this dilemma? Mindfully committing to more peas and less bread if you want a healthy diet. Exactly the same is true with respect to your meaning opportunities.

You will be in a different relationship to each item on your menu of meaning opportunities, respecting some of them but not actually loving them, loving some but not actually respecting them, craving some and finding others a matter of duty. Indeed, your relationship to each may well prove surprisingly complex, encompassing how language operates, what you fell in love with as a child, what you've been told amounts to valuable or meaningful work, and so on.

Because of all this complexity, we must simplify. One way to simplify is to have the following sort of inner conversation: "I need a rich mix of meaning opportunities, since it looks like it will take a rich mix to provide me with both enough meaning and also the right meaning. What is the right mix for me? Let me sort this out and come up with a (of course tentative) mix of meaning opportunities that might work for me."

By having this conversation you move from the idea of a personal menu of meaning opportunities to the idea of a personal mix of meaning opportunities, a refinement that will go a long way toward helping you juggle such quite different meaning opportunities as visiting with your cat, writing your novel, remaining calm at all times, being open to love, switching jobs, doing more gardening, and weaning yourself from the daily news.

You don't want to scorn or devalue the experience of visiting with your cat or enjoying your garden, if those are value-based meaning-making experiences for you. You do not need to say that those "aren't really meaningful," or that they are "shallow meaning opportunities" or that they are "indulgences masquerading as meaning opportunities." Still, engaging in *just* those activities is unlikely to satisfy you, make you proud of your efforts, or amount to a meaningful-enough life. They are real and legitimate but unlikely to prove sufficient.

The question for you to answer is, "What is the right mix for me?" Try answering this question. Look at your menu of meaning opportunities (create it first if you haven't yet done so; see page 27), and try to discern what mix might work for you: which items must appear, which items might appear only occasionally, which items satisfy which values and which satisfy other values. Before you start on this task, however, please read over the next question since that will help you figure out how to proceed. Then come back and tackle creating your mix of meaning opportunities.

The second question you need to address is, "How do I make this mix fit into my real life?"

Let's say you've come up with your tentative mix and it includes a great diversity of items, from being states (like calmness or bravery) to daily tasks (like working on your novel) to periodic tasks (like having Sunday dinner with your mate) to recovery tasks (like not drinking or not surfing the Net) to big-change tasks (like switching careers) to spontaneous tasks (like being open to nature or being open to love). What does this mix look like in real life?

Let's take a look at a hypothetical menu mix of six items that includes writing your novel, being calm at all times, having dinner with your mate three times a week, staying open to love, changing your job, and weaning yourself from the daily news. Remember that at the same time you must deal with your current job, deal with all your other duties and responsibilities, find time to relax, and include everything else that must be included. So, how do you do this? By having a conversation with yourself that sounds something like the following:

"Getting to the novel every day is simple to pencil in: I just put it on my schedule first thing each day before my 'real day' begins. So easy to say! But of course I have to change my habits and deal with everyday resistance just to do this one thing. Okay! So I must figure that out. At the same time I have to pay real attention to switching jobs because my current one is too meaningless and too poorly paid for me to continue in it. So how does that fit into my daily negotiations? Well, I could look for jobs as a regular daily meaning investment. But how do I stay calm through all this, and how on earth do I stay open to love as I'm struggling to write my novel, trying to change jobs, and spending too many hours at my soul-sucking job? Okay, breathe. How do I stay calm and remain open to love in my real circumstances? Well, somehow these being states have to take priority. In some sense being has to take precedence over doing. Maybe this concretely means..." and so on.

This is the sort of conversation to have. Now, time to do the work!

1. Create your mix of meaning opportunities, mindfully chatting with yourself about your rationale for your particular mix.
2. Have the equally important conversation with yourself about how to live this mix while living the rest of life too.

3. When you've done this, live this way for the remainder of the week!

4. At the end of the week, please take a few moments to jot down your thoughts about the experience.

Margaret: No Perfect Timing, No Perfect Plan

Margaret, an artist and businesswoman from Seattle, shared how her beliefs about meaning evolved:

> Thank you so much for all the mind-boggling new ideas of making meaning. In all honesty, reading your theories has shaken my beliefs a bit. I used to think of myself as very free-spirited until I became more aware of how much I was governed by the belief of a universe that has a divine plan for me. This year, the belief of a benevolent or interactive universe has been eroded by some very difficult life changes and health issues, and I'd already begun questioning my spiritual beliefs when I started boot camp.
>
> All of a sudden, I've realized that my beliefs were sapping my energy more than supporting me. Thinking that there must be the perfect purpose for me out there and thinking that if I lived according to spiritual principles then all would be well, I started to get impatient and angry with myself about why I still seem to struggle so much.
>
> Your theory of natural psychology showed me a different way of approaching this dilemma. There isn't perfect timing or a plan out there; instead, there are our complex circumstances, our personality, and our limited time and energy resources. It's up to us to have a conversation about our complex situation

and decide what kind of meanings we want to invest in. So instead of this endless search for "how to best apply myself in life," I can actually decide in what arenas I want to make meaning and what situations and activities will bring opportunities to make meaning, and to also take time-outs from having to make meaning and having to live my purpose.

After my core was shaken, a peaceful state came over me and I started to understand that this approach is more compassionate than my previous one. Before, I thought I wasn't making enough effort. Now I realize I am already putting effort toward my values and am on the right path and therefore can also take the time to relax and also give myself permission to be proud of my efforts.

When creating my menu of meaning opportunities, I was surprised by how many opportunities there are for me to experience meaning, allow for meaning to happen, or actively make meaning. And when I started to plan my days and consciously put these opportunities, such as buying art supplies and showing up in my studio, into my plan for each day, it felt so good to live like this. I realized how much of what I do is already in alignment with my values and that meaning doesn't have to be creating a masterwork every single day. I am more aware of what matters to me and that even simple activities like buying art supplies serve a greater purpose (my development as an artist). At the end of the day, living with this state of mindfulness and intention made me feel much better and proud even of little achievements.

When considering what mix of value-based meaning opportunities I need to invest in so that I have a rich experience of all the things I value, I realized that it will take some trial and error and lots of practice in making meaning in a conscious and mindful way. The first very valuable habit I want to create is the morning meaning check-in. Because I am self-employed and a parent, my daily routine is very fluid, and the check-in allows me to be flexible and to set my intentions according to the specific needs of the upcoming day.

I've created a little morning routine (my check-in about setting intentions and steps for the day), earmarked ninety minutes right after my morning routine for making the most meaning (work on developing my home business), scheduled time during the day for something that I value but that requires less concentrated work (taking a walk, doing yoga, going to an art show, seeing a friend, doing some self-care such as taking a bath), and included a stint before bed when I write a short review of how the day went and what I appreciate about myself and my life.

I've been putting my plan into action for the past six days, and it has worked well most days. I realize that in order to sustain the schedule, I need to keep this very flexible and maintain a long-term vision. Some of my meaning opportunities are not directly translatable into activities. For example, I want to upgrade my personality by increasing my self-esteem and confidence. I found that many of my meaning investments are serving this intention indirectly.

Even this exercise of making value-based meaning serves my intention of increasing my self-esteem because I am realizing how much time and effort I am already putting toward my goals. Before I focused on results and when they were not directly visible, I felt bad. Now I can focus more on the process, and that provides a lot more opportunities to celebrate small achievements.

Genine: Menu Planning

Genine, an artist and personal coach in Minnesota, reported her experience of drawing up a menu:

> One of the ideas that helped me a lot was your example of a literal menu of peas, ice cream, and bread. I used that this week to put together a chart, a menu, really, of different opportunities. I experienced such confusion the first week. It's the kind of confusion I experience when something is reaching me deeply. It is as if I simply do not understand the words and concepts. With this menu, I was able to begin charting out what I found so difficult to do in week 1.
>
> What I discovered (and it supported my thoughts from last week) is that my day is *not* filled with many meaningful activities, opportunities, or investments. I knew this last week on a gut level and was unable to move forward. I have come to understand that my choices and decisions have not been based on my values.
>
> Most of my tasks are either work related or have to do with daily chores and responsibilities. On my menu of meaning opportunities I saw things like visiting with friends, making art, creating workshops, being of service, being the activist I want to be, and other items that I rarely get to. This has been eye-opening and, honestly, very sad. I have been experiencing discontent for some time but just could not put my finger on the source.
>
> My life on the outside looks lovely. But in the first week you talked about a meaning crisis, and that's where I've been, unknowingly, for a while. Taking this menu format, I have

continued to create categories and to place into those categories what really fits. The menu idea has been a breakthrough for me!

This week please work on your menu of meaning opportunities and your mix of meaning opportunities.

WEEK 3

Upgrading Your Personality

I hope you've enjoyed — and maybe already benefitted from — our first two weeks of work, creating your menu and your mix of meaning opportunities. Let's continue! If you want to engage in value-based meaning-making and live your life purposes, which we will begin to name and frame in a few weeks, you will first need to do two things. You will need to become a person who is equal to doing this work, and you will need to put yourself in a position to do this work. The first involves what I call "upgrading your personality," and the second involves dealing with, and maybe changing,

your circumstances. Next week we will examine your circumstances; this week we look at upgrading your personality.

Your Three Personalities

We are all born with a personality — our original personality, so to speak. Every parent knows that her children are
born with their own idiosyncratic personalities, just as anyone who has ever watched kittens or puppies knows that each
comes with an individual personality. Oddly enough, traditional psychologies and philosophies do not posit or credit
birth differences — but in natural psychology we do.

That isn't to say, however, that we can *know* what our
original personality is or was. There are many things we just
don't know about, and this is one of them. We may *feel* as
if we know what sort of person we were at birth or who we
were supposed to become, but we can never know for certain if that feeling is accurate or an artifact of our formed
personality.

Still, the fact that we *are* each born different is both the-
oretically and practically important, even if we can't identify
those differences. That we are each born different alerts us
to the fact that every human being may start out with very
different ideas about what matters — and therefore with very
different constructions of meaning. Meaning, like all our
psychological experiences, will always be subjective, idiosyncratic, and personal rather than objective, universal, and one
size fits all; and who we are subjectively must connect somehow to our original personality.

If, for example, little Jane was born sadder and wiser

than little Johnny, then it will be normal for her to be sadder and wiser throughout her life; and that original endowment will poignantly affect her experience of meaning. She may feel miserable a lot of the time, and she may have more trouble keeping meaning afloat than the next person. She is not abnormal; she is simply playing out her birth instructions, just as little Johnny is playing out his birth instructions when he learns to tie his shoelaces or to ride his bicycle.

No one, including Jane herself, can know what Jane's original personality consisted of. This is one of our existential realities. We just can't know. Even if you asked some objective observer, say, your uncle Max, what you were like when you were born, and he replied that you were happy-go-lucky or withdrawn, would that amount to an answer? Certainly it wouldn't.

It wouldn't for two reasons. First, no observer could know what was going on inside you or could gauge how, for example, your cheerfulness masked your sadness or your flightiness masked your boredom. Second, even if you could nail down that you had been happy-go-lucky or withdrawn at birth, you would still not know if you were supposed to *remain that way*; that is, you would still not know anything about your particular blueprint or, to use fanciful language, your particular destiny.

As you can see, the phrase *original personality* has two different ideas built into it: that you were already a certain sort of person when you were born, and that you had a developmental path built into you when you were born. Even if you could discern the first, say, through home movies and the reports of relatives, you would not be able to ever know the second.

This isn't to say, however, that because we can't know these things we must come to a screeching halt in our understanding of what could now help us achieve our goals or relieve our distress. No: because your ability to be the person you would like to be hinges more on the *use you make of your available personality* than on the contours of your *original personality* or your *formed personality*. Your available personality is yours to heal, change, grow, and make meaning with.

It is probably wise to let go of any fascination we may have with our original personality, except perhaps in a few regards, say, with regard to our sexual orientation and our innate intelligence. We also want to let go of any fear that our formed personality is too rigid to allow us to make meaning. Instead, we focus on how our available personality permits us to align our life with our principles and our intentions. This focus on available personality and the effort to make use of it returns us to the vibrant present, where we can actively work on the project of our life.

To sum up, we come with an original personality about which we will never know enough; a formed personality that amounts to our rote, mechanical ways of operating; and an available personality that is our remaining freedom. This simple idea allows for a generous world of complexity. It allows for the idea that on a given day we may be pulled by our original personality in ways that disturb us and perplex us. It allows for the idea that, to soothe ourselves and to reduce our anxiety, we might fall prey to an addiction or a compulsion as a feature of our formed personality. It allows for the idea that with our available personality we can work to reduce our defensiveness and alter our habits of mind. This simple model allows for all sorts of sophisticated conversations about our complex reality.

Most people function well enough day to day. As complicated as human beings are psychologically, most simplify and reduce their complicated nature into rote days punctuated by work, some entertainment, some sadness and worries, and the relatively uneventful passage of sixteen hours from sunrise to bedtime. Their formed personality has been formed to allow them to do exactly this, to open their shop or sit down at their cubicle at 8:00 AM, deal with their customers, and modulate their sadness even as they think about the warm weather. This does not quite amount to a life of quiet desperation, but it *is* a life of mind-numbing routine punctuated by sadness, boredom, and nightmares, a life that rises above the level of misery but falls far short of meaningful.

Most of us, whatever culture and circumstances we find ourselves in, maneuver in exactly this normal, limited way, propelled by habits of mind, defenses, and formed personality through days that feel safe enough because they have been measured for safety and good enough because they include just enough pleasure: a decent sandwich at lunch, an amusing television show in the evening, a soothing round of Internet surfing or shopping or drinking. This allows us to function in society and to tolerate life.

Many millions of people live less functionally than this and spend most or all of their day thwarted by their formed personality. The severity of their loss of freedom is greater than average. These thwarted folks may have less control over their anger and live in a perpetual rage; less control over their drinking and live in an alcoholic haze; less control over their fantasizing and never leave their inner world; less control over their dangerous habits and compulsively seek risks and adrenaline rushes.

Put simply, the man who has a glass of wine at lunch to soothe himself, even though he has reasons not to have that glass of wine and even though he would prefer not to have it, is in conflict with himself but is living functionally enough. The man who has six glasses of wine at lunch, whose day is organized around drinking and who is hiding his habit, is living a thwarted day. In terms of our model, the person living a thwarted day has even less available personality at his disposal than the person living a functional day and so will have to stretch further if he wants to engage in value-based meaning-making.

If you think of available freedom in terms of amount, then you want to use some as is and reclaim some from your formed personality. Consider this analogy. You are a farmer, you become aware of the popularity of a certain crop, and you see that it would serve you to plant that crop. However, all your fields except a few are taken up with other crops. You have a certain amount of land available for your new crop. But you also have other land that over time you could turn over to this new crop.

In the same sense you have a certain amount of available personality, and you can increase your available personality by mindfully upgrading your formed personality. These twin activities of making use of your available personality and upgrading your formed personality so as to reclaim *more* available personality are among your prime meaning opportunities. In other words, *you* are your prime meaning opportunity.

Tips for Upgrading Your Personality

Here are eight tips for turning you into someone better able to make value-based meaning:

Find the Right Language

First, you need a way to talk to yourself about your available personality and your formed personality. If you don't create that way of speaking, you won't know what you now have available for meaning-making purposes or what aspects of your formed personality you want to upgrade.

One way to chat about these matters is to use the language of freedom. This might sound like, "I believe that I'm free to form strong intentions. But I don't think that I'm free yet to consistently align my thoughts with the intentions I form. I have sufficient freedom to form an intention but not sufficient freedom to keep my mind focused on and aligned with that intention. That is the aspect of my personality that I most want to upgrade. To that end I am going to keep a 'thought alignment' notebook and keep serious track of what I'm thinking and how well my thoughts align with my intentions."

You need to decide how you'll talk to yourself about your available personality and your formed personality. If you can't come up with the language, you're less likely to have the conversation.

Address Your Defensiveness

You will want to deal directly and heroically with your defensiveness, one of the ways that we most reduce our self-awareness and limit our freedom. *Defensiveness*, a word that Freud introduced and that his daughter Anna explored extensively, is a lovely, useful term that stands for the many ways we refuse to deal with the facts of existence, our circumstances, and the shadows of our personalities.

People tend to reflexively defend themselves in a score of characteristic ways, ways with names like denial, intellectualization, projection, rationalization, repression, sublimation, and so on. These are very smart psychoanalytic ideas and completely compatible with natural psychology. But we must not make too much use of these defense mechanisms.

If you are busily defending yourself against self-knowledge, isn't it also impossible to gain self-knowledge? Yes and no. As much as we pull the wool over our eyes, gaps remain through which we can see our antics. We must use those gaps. That is the very essence of making use of our available personality. You announce as loudly as you can that while it may prove difficult, you are going to heroically examine your defensiveness and work to reduce it. In this way you make use of your available personality in reducing your defensiveness.

Unless you're familiar with the technical language of defense mechanisms, you'll have to chat with yourself in everyday language. This might sound like the following: "How do I defend myself? Well, I think I hide things from myself. Even though I knew that my novel needed another revision,

I sort of hid that knowledge from myself and blamed the fact that I couldn't get it published on the publishing industry. So there's that. And because I'm pretty clever I dream up extremely imaginative ways of talking myself into wasting whole years on oddball pursuits, when I know I should be doing something else. So I guess that my prime defenses are hiding things from myself and cleverly misleading myself."

Have this chat with yourself even though, being defended, you don't really want to!

Recognize Your Counterproductive Habits of Mind

You will want to pay attention to your habits of mind and make use of your available personality to reduce the grip of your habitual thinking.

Not all our habitual thinking is a problem. It is not a problem to remember that there are twelve inches to a foot, that you enjoyed swimming at the lake when you were ten, or that you prefer your asparagus crisp. However, it *is* a problem to identify yourself as untalented, to hold a grudge against the universe for not making it easier on you, and to go directly to rage when you're feeling slighted.

How easy will it be for you to seize relationships as meaning opportunities if you lead with criticism? How easy will it be for you to seize performing as a meaning opportunity if your mental habits provoke anxiety at the thought of performing? Your habitual ways of thinking can prevent you from seizing your most important meaning opportunities. Which of your habits of mind need your attention?

Appraise Your Ideas and Emotions

You will want to stop paying yourself the inadvertent compliment of believing that every idea you have is a good one simply because it came to you. Nor do you want to take every feeling that arises in you seriously just because it arose in you. To the extent that these thoughts and feelings arise from your formed personality, you must appraise them with your available personality so that you can judge if you really want to countenance them.

You do not have to write a novel because a fascinating idea for a novel just passed through your mind. What you want to do instead is to judge with your available personality how much sense it makes to write that novel. You do not need to descend into despair because your feelings just got deeply hurt. What you want to do instead is to judge how much you want to allow those feelings to open the door to pain and darkness. You will have more luck with making meaning if you do not let the liveliness and powerfulness of ideas and emotions cause you to accept them without appraisal. Remember that a strong emotion is just a strong emotion and that a clever idea is just a clever idea: neither are mandates.

Appreciate and Use Your Strengths

Some aspects of your formed personality are strengths, and you will want to manifest these strengths and to count on them. Not everything about your formed personality is a problem. We should prize and maintain those aspects of our formed personality that we respect. You have many ways of doing things and many ways of being that have become automatic over the years — smiling that certain smile, growing tenacious in the face of difficulty, leading with fairness — that you like and respect about yourself. Keep being *that* person.

Reevaluate Your Values

Some values and principles you want to uphold, but others you may want to minimize or eliminate. If you're a rock musician who values being stoned, that is a value you will probably want to reevaluate and de-value. If you're a lawyer holding it as a principle that "unless I put in more hours than my colleagues I'll never succeed," and you realize that you're ruining your health and your home life by following that principle, that is a principle that you will probably want to reevaluate and de-value. The practice of making value-based meaning includes using your available personality to ensure that you really value your values.

Create and Regulate Your Identity

You will want to create an identity that serves you. Creating that identity is its own meaning opportunity. How we identify ourselves affects how we live. If, for example, you intend to compose music but refuse to internally identify yourself as a composer, you will find it much more difficult to write songs. If you identify yourself as someone who "doesn't do well on the road," you may talk yourself out of your workshop career or your performing career. If you identify yourself as someone with "the mental disorder of depression," when in fact you are unhappy and not mentally ill, that self-identification can weaken you and send you in the direction of chemical fixes, which you may or may not need. How you identify yourself matters.

You will want to create good, strong identifications that serve you. At the same time you will want to retain the flexibility to disidentify from a given identity piece if doing so serves you. Creating and regulating your identity are among your prime meaning opportunities. If you confidently identify yourself as a calm person, the hero of your own story, and equal to your challenges, you have just like that made some value-based meaning!

Notice How Your Circumstances Affect You

The amount of available personality at your disposal is not so much a precise or a static amount as it is a contextual amount. You have more of it available in situations that promote freedom and less of it available in situations that restrict your freedom. For example, it may be in you to be a compassionate person — that may be a significant feature of your available personality. But if you are suddenly thrust into the role of prison guard, as were the Stanford University students who participated in Philip Zimbardo's famous experiment in which students were divided into "prisoners" and "guards," in a matter of minutes you may find significantly less compassion available to you.

Kind people can become sadists, rational people can become irrational, fair-minded people can become selfish, all in no time, if the circumstances are severe or powerful enough. Noticing how situations reduce your ability to manifest your available personality is its own sort of meaning opportunity. You might, for example, notice how a certain advertising campaign is manipulating you into wanting to buy something that you do not want or need — that noticing will itself feel meaningful. The amount of available personality at your disposal increases or decreases according to your circumstances. Remembering that fact is its own meaning opportunity!

If meaning were out there somewhere, if it were an objective reality of some sort, then we wouldn't need to improve ourselves in order to possess it. We would simply hunt for it, wait for it, open the door and invite it in, without needing to change ourselves as we hunt or wait. But since we must *make* our own meaning if we are to possess the meaning we crave, we need to transform ourselves into the sort of person *equal* to that making. That is our work and a significant part of the project of our lives.

Your Work for the Week

First let me describe your work for the week in a very cumbersome way. You begin by saying, "I am going to employ my available personality to upgrade my formed personality so that I can make value-based meaning without getting in my own way, without doubting my new intentions, and without backsliding into any misunderstandings about the nature, location, or availability of meaning. I know what I need to know about making value-based meaning, and now I need to be the 'me' who makes myself proud by my efforts and who makes value-based meaning every day. This week I will work on becoming more of that sort of person in the following ways." Then you name those ways and live them.

Now let me say it in a much simpler way: you are transforming yourself into a savvy value-based meaning-maker. Work on this transformation this week! In one sense this isn't work at all but rather a supersized shift in your way of being that allows you to continually and effortlessly move from one "next right thing" to another. That next right thing might be a meaning opportunity, a chore, a meaning-neutral period, or some relaxing activity. If you can accomplish this effortless moving from one right thing to another, you will have upgraded your personality without much heavy lifting.

In another sense, it is indeed work. You may need to carefully identify what you want to upgrade (which may be more than one thing), get clear on how you'll accomplish that upgrading, connect that work to your ongoing work of creating (and living) your personal mix of meaning opportunities, and then do the work you name for yourself. Remember, this is boot camp!

To help organize your thoughts (and you can use these as writing prompts for the end of the week), you might try your hand at answering the following three questions.

1. What, if anything, about your personality did you decide needed upgrading?
2. How did you translate that into actual work? What did you do to upgrade your personality?
3. If you made the effort to upgrade your personality, how did that affect your meaning-making efforts?

Mary: A Calm Bonus

Mary, a journalist from Illinois, described shedding a bad habit as part of her upgrade:

> I decided that one badly needed and hopefully very beneficial personality upgrade that I want to work on is getting to and from places on time. When I was a journalist, I never missed a deadline. But in real life I often try to pack too many tasks in before I need either to get writing or to leave the house for an appointment. As a result, I am always running just a few minutes late. For sure, I am never early. I then have to apologize or explain why I was late.
>
> I figure if I can get a handle on being early, I will waste less time and emotional energy on something stupid and so easily within my control. That will give me more energy to follow my meaning-based pursuits. I know how to do this: getting things laid out the night before, not taking a phone call when I don't really want to talk to someone, excusing myself from a conversation when I know I should be somewhere else. I just need to do it!
>
> I teach this to my kids. But to achieve my new goal I am going to seriously have to change my thought patterns, those patterns that enter my brain whenever I have somewhere to go. I need to realize that in the name of getting a few more things done around the house or on my computer I am really procrastinating or am actually anxious about doing the next thing. Anxious, I rev myself up, distract myself, do "one last thing," and fail to get where I'm going on time.
>
> I want to start getting to places on time. I think that would

produce a calm bonus that would begin to reduce my overall experience of anxiety. That's my personality upgrade goal.

Barbara: Throwing the Switch on My Life Energy

Barbara, a whole-foods cook and educator from Portland, Oregon, reported on the two personality upgrades that she wanted to undertake:

For the most part, and in order to keep things doable, I focused on two upgrades that I've been working on for a few years now. One was watching my thoughts and changing them. The other was throwing the switch on my life energy or passion.

It's been a busy week with lots going on. For the most part I was more mindful of my thoughts, and also more accepting. There simply *are* a lot of dull, boring, repetitive thoughts running through my head. So instead of changing every one of those thoughts, I just accepted them. This past year I've been trying to think bigger, which for me meant replacing not only negative thoughts but boring, dull, repetitive thoughts as well. Because really, how many times do I need to think about what I'm having for supper? But it didn't really help to try to replace every thought I had with a "bigger" thought — that simply made me tired. So this week I worked on accepting my routine thoughts while trying to *add* some bigger thoughts to the mix.

Upping my passion and life energy turned out to be fun. I had the opportunity to spend time with a couple of passionate people this week, and that increased my passion and energy. What I noticed, not for the first time, is that a lot of people live with the switch turned on medium and just as many live with it on low. Of course, we need to be mindful of where other people are at in order to have rapport with them, but when I try to turn up the passion and energy with these folks I just feel out of sync with them. This week I realized (again) that it's really important for me to have fun, passionate people in my life, people who want to explore, who want more joy in their lives, who have goals and dreams and want to reach them.

Deciding that I truly matter has changed how I approach everything in my life, which, without my doing anything else, turns out to be a meaning booster!

Bring your available personality to bear on your formed personality, name the personality upgrade you want to make, and give that work a serious try this week. Remember why you are doing this work: because you want to turn yourself into the person equal to living your life purposes. Any upgrade you make — or even begin to make — supports that intention.

WEEK 4

Dealing with Your Circumstances

Our ability to live our life purposes and to make meaning is profoundly affected by our circumstances. You must live in the crucible of reality, and you must factor your circumstances into your calculations about life.

Part of us wants to skip noticing our circumstances, contriving to lead a life of fantasy. Who can say if some psychotic breaks aren't the efforts of overtaxed individuals to quit with reality and withdraw into permanent fantasy? What child hasn't gone to his room and shut out reality by turning the music up loud? All of us sometimes wish that we could put our life circumstances on hold, or even make them go away. The extreme existential playing out of this desire is suicide.

Another part of us wants to live, and not only live but lead a principled life in which we make value-based meaning. We want to get from life what we can, including small pleasures and quiet relaxations. That part of us knows exactly how much avoiding reality will doom our meaning-making efforts. Even a monk who has joined a cloistered community where his circumstances are reduced to essentials knows, if his ethical radar is working, that what goes on outside the walls of his monastery matters. The part of us that would like to make ourselves proud knows that reality matters.

If that monk comfortably meditates while his brothers and sisters live in tyranny and poverty just outside the gates of the monastery, that is certainly his right. Each of us is the arbiter of our own meaning. Nothing in the universe will dispute his decision or call him to account. A cloistered monk or an addict on a perpetual high can find his ways of not dealing with reality. But your meaning-making efforts, informed by your values and principles, are pretty likely to demand that you deal with reality as forthrightly as you can.

It follows that dealing forthrightly with the circumstances of your life *becomes* one of your prime meaning opportunities and one of your major life purposes. The phrase *making value-based meaning* implies an active and intentional relationship with reality and has embedded in it the idea that meaning can only be made in the midst of your circumstances. Your life purposes, however you go about naming and framing them, ought likewise to have embedded in them this essential truth: that reality matters.

Looking Truth in the Eye

Unfortunately, you can't deal with your circumstances solely by adopting a certain attitude or by getting a good grip on your mind. Both of these are important skills to master, and our mind does make much of our misery. The more you think thoughts that serve you and adopt an attitude that serves you, the less misery you'll experience. But you must also *deal* with your circumstances and not just change your mind about them or adopt a certain attitude toward them. Our values and our principles demand that we participate in the affairs of the world and deal with the world.

Your life purposes are inexorably connected to the facts of existence. However, they are connected to them in very complicated ways. Consider the following example. Say that you've identified as one of your life purposes the purpose of telling truth to power. As it happens, your country is taken over by a tyrant. In a way, this is a golden opportunity for you to manifest one of your life purposes. In an equally obvious way these are also dreadful circumstances, both for your country and for you personally. If you decide to tell truth to that tyrant, you will face dire consequences. How might you handle that moment, knowing that your voice was *never more needed* and likewise knowing how *catastrophically dangerous* it will be to speak up?

This is exactly the kind of predicament that reality presents us with. It presents us with illnesses, failed relationships, blows in the marketplace, career missteps, cataclysmic global events, and every manner of obstacle, from water heaters breaking to bullies abusing our kids. Innumerable hard realities come with living one's life purposes. We look this truth in the eye — and we help ourselves deal with our circumstances by forthrightly addressing the following seven questions (which we will return to in simplified form on page 84).

The first is, "Do I understand my circumstances? Do I step back regularly, and have I stepped back recently, to investigate my situation?" Most people, even those who chat with themselves via journaling or some other way, find life rushing by too quickly to ever really know what their circumstances *are*. You can change this dynamic by putting some system into place that helps you keep track of your life's realities.

The second question is, "Which of my circumstances do I really hate looking at?" Can I look squarely at those difficult circumstances? Maybe the boringness of your job is the thing you find hardest to look at directly. Maybe it's your alcohol or drug use. Maybe it's your chronic poverty, which affects everything from your ability to stay healthy to your ability to keep up your spirits. These are not easy things to look at. But not looking at the circumstances that hold us down is a poorer plan.

Our third question helps you discriminate between those circumstances that are important to consider and those that aren't: "Do these particular circumstances actually affect my ability to live my life purposes?" It may annoy you that your neighbors are building an addition that partially blocks your view. However, does their addition affect your ability to live your life purposes? If it's just annoying, let it go. It may sadden you that winter where you live lasts eight months. If that dreary winter does affect your ability to live your life purposes, you must at a minimum buy a sun lamp. But if it doesn't, ignore it. Many things that upset us, sadden us, or make us anxious may not be things that genuinely affect our ability to live our life purposes. If they aren't, let them go!

Our fourth question is, "Might a new attitude toward my circumstances help me do a better job of living my life purposes?" Might it pay you to have a calmer, more philosophical, more detached perspective of many of your circumstances? For those circumstances that do matter a lot, might it pay to adopt a more passionate, energetic attitude? What attitudes should you adopt according to the exact circumstances you face?

Our fifth question is, "How can I go about changing those circumstances that are negatively affecting me?" We can't control a storm raging through our neighborhood or a storm of illness raging through our community. We can't single-handedly repair the ozone layer. But we can ask ourselves, with respect to any of our circumstances, "Are these among the circumstances that I *can* improve?" If you don't regularly ask that question, you won't give yourself the chance to positively affect those circumstances that *would* allow you to help yourself.

Our sixth question is, "What new circumstances are looming on the horizon, and how proactive should I be about them?" Just as an approaching hurricane might cause you to repair your storm shutters, if a change in your circumstances is coming your way, there may be smart things for you to do *right now* to prepare. If, for example, you are moving to Spain, you might want to start learning some Spanish right now. Planning ahead is obviously a good thing — but how many people actually do it?

Our seventh question is, "Do I have a system for communicating with myself about my circumstances and keeping track of them?" What mechanisms will you use to keep track of your shifting circumstances and of the efforts you are making to influence your circumstances? Will you use a daily planner or some technological equivalent? Will you check in with yourself the same time each day or the same time each week? It is one thing to agree that your circumstances matter and another to make the time and effort to look at your circumstances systematically.

Our ability to manifest our life purposes is inexorably tied to the nature of our circumstances and our ability to deal with those circumstances. If one of your life purposes is to write novels, it matters whether anybody is publishing novels and whether anybody is reading novels. If one of your life purposes is to enjoy your family, it matters whether your grandchildren are down the block or ten thousand miles away. If one of your life purposes is to speak freely, it matters to what extent you are censored or encouraged to speak. To imagine that we can live our life purposes independent of reality is, well, fantasy. The more you look that painful reality in the eye, the more you will be living authentically.

Your Meaning Repair Kit

One of our profound and enduring circumstances is the way that meaning comes and goes.

Since meaning is "just" a psychological experience of a certain sort, it is natural that it comes and goes. You can't have joy every minute; you can't have meaning every minute. In one sense this is no problem. You maturely accept that there must be times, even protracted and unpleasant times, when you are not experiencing life as meaningful. Still, it can feel terrible to live without meaning for too long. Learning how to deal with *that* circumstance, that you are being terrorized by the absence of meaning, is vitally important.

What will you do if either too much time passes without life feeling meaningful or a meaning crisis hits? Well, you might pull out your meaning repair kit and repair meaning. Think of a sewing kit. It contains only a small number of items — a thimble, some needles, some threads of various colors, a few generic buttons — but with it you can repair a garment. It is simplicity itself. Your meaning repair kit is as simple as that. In it are six items named so that the word *repair* becomes an acronym: a reminder bell, an evaluator themometer, a personality tap, an aligner level, an investment planner, and a reality tester.

Your Reminder Bell

Let's look at the first item. When you experience a meaning crisis of any sort, small or large, you grab your meaning repair kit, take out your reminder bell, jingle it, and remind yourself of the nature of meaning. You remind yourself that whatever subjective experience you are having, including the feeling that meaning has vanished, is just a subjective experience. Ringing your bell reminds you that you are still committed to making value-based meaning.

You jingle your bell and remind yourself that any confusion, doubt, revulsion, or pain you are experiencing is part of the process of being human and that despite *what you are feeling* you will confidently return to value-based meaning-making. Maybe the confluence of your job not mattering enough, your primary relationship falling apart, your formed personality dragging you down, and your bills piling up is conspiring to produce an earthquake-sized meaning crisis. You jingle your reminder bell and remind yourself that this is only a *crisis* and not a *repudiation* of your understanding that your life is your ongoing project.

Your Evaluator Thermometer

Next you make sure that this crisis hasn't altered your view of life. To do this you use the second item in your meaning repair kit, your evaluator thermometer. You use this thermometer to gauge whether or not you are evaluating life as worth living and your efforts as mattering. When a meaning crisis strikes, not only do we feel bereft of meaning, but we may also recalibrate our evaluation of life downward, like downgrading a stock from A to C, and experience life as cold. You use your evaluator thermometer to see if that unfortunate and unnecessary downgrading has happened. If it *has* happened, if your thermometer indicates that your taste for life has fallen below zero, you remind yourself that life still matters. Give your circumstances a C, if you like; but give life its A back.

It is one thing to discover that your lover is cheating on you or to suddenly doubt the profession you chose. These are tremendously painful events and create crises of meaning. But you do not have to make the leap from feeling this pain to announcing that life itself is worthless, that you are taking your ball and going home, that the project of your life is over.

You do not have to go *there,* and your evaluator thermometer is the tool you use to see if you have.

Your Personality Tap

Next you grab your personality tap and tap into your available personality to make the necessary repairs. Picture your personality tap as a sort of miniature mallet. You tap yourself, maybe tapping your wrist or your palm, ritualistically reminding yourself that you have enough personality available with which to make new meaning.

You tap, tap, tap and say, "I know that my job is sucking the life out of me and leaving me with little energy to make the changes that I know I need to make. This has produced one heck of a meaning crisis. But I *also* know that I have enough personality available to make the necessary changes. I also have skills and strengths to bring from my formed personality and acres of formed personality to reclaim in the service of making these repairs." You tap, tap, tap, and as you tap you mobilize your personality for the work to come.

Your Aligner Level

The fourth item in your meaning repair kit is an aligner level. This instrument helps you realign your thoughts and actions with your intentions. At the left end of the level are your intentions. At the right end are your thoughts and actions. When you are standing behind your intentions and when you have aligned your thoughts and actions with those intentions, the bubble marker of your level moves to the middle, and you are existentially centered.

When a meaning crisis strikes, you are bound to fall out of level, and your aligner level alerts you to that imbalance. Your level works in the following way. When the bubble moves to the left, that means your intentions need readjusting. When it moves to the right, that means your thoughts or actions aren't aligned with your intentions. Say, for example, that your strong intention was to spend your life as a social worker but your current meaning crisis has put that choice into question. The bubble of your aligner level moves to the left, alerting you to the fact that your very *intention* is now in question.

Maybe your intention still holds but your thoughts are failing to serve you because of the crisis. Say, for example, that it remains your intention to start a home business but a financial crisis has struck and you need to take a day job. Now you're pestered by thoughts like, "If only I'd worked harder last year my business would be making money today and I wouldn't have to take some stupid day job."

This crisis is producing thoughts that don't serve you, and those thoughts are making the crisis worse. Your aligner level alerts you to this fact as the bubble moves to the right. Observing its position, you know to get a grip on your mind and realign your thoughts with your intentions. This might sound like, "My intention remains the same. I'll get a day job, but I'm going to work on my online business two hours every day!" This conversation helps move the bubble back toward the center. You likewise use your level to see if your actions are appropriately aligned with your intentions. This snappy device helps you keep your intentions up-to-date and your thoughts and actions aligned with your updated intentions.

Your Investment Planner

The fifth item in your meaning repair kit is an investment planner. You use it to jot down the meaning investments you intend to make as part of this particular repair. Say that loneliness has caused a meaning crisis. You jot down in your investment planner that you are going to investigate online dating services, join local meet-up groups, reconnect with some friends, or go out at lunch rather than sit at your desk. You use your investment planner to plan and schedule concrete actions that serve your intentions and that you intuit will help you repair meaning.

Your Reality Tester

The sixth and last item in your meaning repair kit is a reality tester. You use it to ensure that the repairs you intend to make square with the facts of existence. Say that you stare up at the night sky, experience a meaning crisis because of some fleeting thought about your mortality, and get it into your head that you would like to make a meaning investment in interstellar travel. No matter how well you align your thoughts with this intention, you will not pull off this feat. You use your reality tester to help you form reality-based intentions and to identify the plausible things you might try in order to realize those intentions.

It would be nice to be able to meet a meaning crisis in a split second rather than having to do the heavy lifting of actual repair. Sometimes you can. Sometimes you can bring yourself back with a sigh, a laugh, or a tiny reminder. There will be other times, however, when the crisis is powerful and profound, when it feels less like a button popping off your shirt and more like the whole fabric ripping. Then you will need to pull out your meaning repair kit. Those circumstances dictate it!

Your Work for the Week

Your work this week is investigative. I do not expect you to change any of your circumstances, although if you see a way to do that and want to attempt it, that would be lovely! Rather, I see your work as trying to answer the seven questions I posed above so that, maybe for the first time, you investigate your circumstances in a systematic way.

Here they are again, slightly restated:

1. What are my circumstances? How can I describe them to myself in a simple, efficient way so that I can discern what's working and what needs changing?
2. Which of my circumstances do I really hate looking at? Can I make myself look squarely at those difficult circumstances for the sake of the life I want?
3. Do I spend a lot of my time thinking about (and maybe worrying and complaining about) certain circumstances that don't actually affect my ability to live my life purposes and that I should forget about?
4. Might a new attitude toward my circumstances help me do a better job of living my life purposes? What

attitude should I adopt that would help me better deal with my circumstances?

5. How can I change or positively influence the circumstances that are negatively affecting me? Can I create a plan for changing or positively influencing them?

6. What new circumstances are looming on the horizon, and how proactive should I be about them?

7. Can I create a simple way of communicating with myself about and keeping track of my circumstances?

Try to answer these seven questions. Writing even just a little in response to each will really serve you.

Susan: Busting Out Adventure Girl

Susan, a freelance writer and editor from Minnesota, described her dissatisfaction at work:

My circumstances are fairly good compared to those of most people. I earned a decent income this year from freelancing, I have the luxury of working from home, I have health insurance through my spouse, and my expenses are few.

However, I don't find much satisfaction in the work I do. I love the pay and the fact that it allows me to do the things I want and have the things I want. But I sometimes feel that my talents are being wasted and that I could be doing more and better things, casting a wider net, and making a difference in the world.

I hope that by continuing to follow the principles of this meaning-making boot camp I can begin to sprinkle my life with more meaning opportunities, which I hope will lead to a grander life of service to humanity and the planet. Tall order, I know.

A few things are hard for me to look at. For years I've kvetched about not being paid enough. Finally I landed a well-paying contract, and I can barely bring myself to do the work because I'd rather be doing almost anything else. Because I've worked so hard to make my current situation a reality, and because it's paid off, I don't want to think about having to start over with another career. Writing and editing is what I do professionally, although I'm good at other things, and those other things might (I say *might*) bring me more satisfaction. However, I don't have the credentials in those other things and would have to work even harder to break into another line of work. If I were twenty years younger, no problem! So I feel stuck.

I've resented the fact that I have yet to make a living from my creative writing (as opposed to business writing), which would be my ideal life-supporting venture. I also know that I haven't worked hard enough at making that creative writing life a reality and instead have pursued easier money. So it's hard for me to accept that I haven't done the hard work where my creative life is concerned, and I wonder if I have it in me anymore.

I also don't like looking at the fact that though I've had quite an exciting life full of international travel and adventure, the past few years have been pretty low-key (read: boring). I'd like to once again bust out Adventure Girl, but this time I want something different for her. Rather than using her as my exit strategy to avoid the hard work of life — as I've done in the past — I want her to lead me down a path of making more meaning. But I don't know how to do that, and I don't feel like my circumstances would allow for it, even if I knew what it meant.

What do I spend a lot of time thinking about that doesn't really serve me? Having a perfect house, organizing everything, and getting annoyed by having to work to pay the bills. I'm too preoccupied with busyness to focus either on work that pays the bills or on work that brings me joy. Does my house really have to be ready for a *Better Homes and Gardens* photo shoot? Can't I function if the dishes linger in the sink for a day or if the receipts aren't filed? Do I even *need* to keep receipts? I know that these things are petty, and I'd like to forget about them!

I think an attitude of gratefulness would help. I *am* grateful, and I do give thanks every day for what I have. I just have to remind myself that I've worked hard to create what I have — I asked for this. All things considered, my circumstances are pretty good; I just need to learn how to balance what I need with what I want and to not allow either to sabotage my ultimate goal of living life with joy. I also need to adopt the attitude that joy can be found in doing the necessities of life.

How can I go about changing or positively influencing the circumstances that are negatively affecting me? I find that regular meditation on the Divine works. In that meditation I try to bathe the undesirables of my life in white light. My bigger mind knows that all the "bad" stuff is no more than a label I've chosen. My plan would be to meditate daily, which I don't do currently.

What new circumstances are looming on the horizon, and how proactive should I be about them? In less than a year the well-paying contract I have will expire and I'll need to find more work. I fear going back to scrambling for little jobs to make ends meet and praying that another big contract will land on my desk. However, I'm a big believer in the concept that we create our reality simply by what we believe. I've proven that concept pretty clearly throughout my life. So the proactive part for me is to keep the nay-saying demons out of my head and continue heading down a path that includes not just *thinking* thoughts that serve me but also *living* thoughts that serve me.

This week your job is to look your circumstances in the eye. Please attempt this work even if you feel resistant, and even if it makes you anxious. Next week you'll be rewarded with your first look at your life purposes!

WEEK 5
Naming Your Life Purposes

We started boot camp with an investigation of meaning rather than of life purpose. I wanted to get across that meaning is a certain sort of *experience*, whereas life purpose is a certain sort of *intention*. In the first two weeks you worked to increase your experience of meaning by learning to seize meaning opportunities and make meaning investments. You worked in week 3 to upgrade your personality so as to be better equipped to meet your meaning needs. In week 4 you investigated your circumstances to better position yourself to make meaning and decide on your life purposes. Now, in week 5, it's time to name and frame your life purposes.

Your life purposes are your intentions, based on and aligned with your values and your principles. Naming and framing your life purposes will occupy us for the next three weeks, so please don't worry if not everything becomes clear or settled this week. We can take our time with this!

Let's go over some key points.

- The universe does not provide you with life purposes. You must name, embrace, and commit to life purposes of your own choosing.
- We are built to want life to feel valuable and meaningful, but we are also built with many other needs, desires, and attributes, including the ability to self-sabotage and to live carelessly. On any given day you could do nothing in particular, or you could live according to your life purposes. Every human being has that choice to make.
- We are free to thoughtfully consider our relationship to meaning and value, and we are also free to thoughtfully consider our relationship to everything else that life has to offer, from how much television to watch to how much Scotch to drink to how much courage to display. Others may tell us (or may have told us) how to do all that, but they have no right to arbitrate for us. We arbitrate our way of life.
- Each individual comes with a particular personality, a particular psychological makeup, particular psychological experiences, and particular circumstances. There is no way to be "no one." Each of us is someone. This someone has his strengths, weaknesses, insights, blind spots, freedom, lack of freedom, and all the rest.

- You can accept or reject that it is your job to figure out how you will live, that your life is your project, and that only you can decide how to define the project that is your life.
- You can take the reality that life provides us with no purposes except those we decide to name and embrace to mean anything: that therefore life is worthless; that therefore you are free to be selfish and ruthless; that therefore you are free to be careless and not give life much thought; that therefore you are obliged to live according to your vision of a good life; that therefore you intend to spend your time being a value-based meaning-maker.
- You can decide not to give life purpose another moment's thought. Or you can conclude that you are deeply interested in thinking about it — right now. All sorts of conclusions are possible. If you decide you are interested, let's proceed!

How *Not* to Frame Your Life Purposes

How should you name and frame your life purposes? Let's start by looking at several ways that probably would not serve you very well.

1. Avoid naming a single outcome. First, you probably don't want to name a life purpose that requires a certain outcome, unless you also add how you intend to live irrespective of that outcome.

A life purpose such as "writing great novels and having them published" is lovely, but it is also narrow and can prove a painful albatross if you find yourself being held hostage to that single purpose or if it never comes true. The same is true of becoming a bridge builder, training as a concert pianist, playing professional basketball, or flying jets. A single outcome-driven life purpose is a trap.

It takes longer and is more cumbersome to say, "I intend to write great novels and strive to get them published, and I also intend to make meaning in many other ways," but it also serves you much better. It suggests a way of living that is more likely to provide you with satisfaction and emotional health. Think through how much sense it makes to name one specific thing and *only* that thing as your life purpose.

2. Avoid naming a specific way of being. Second is the matter of naming a specific way of being. It can feel simple and sensible to name as your life purpose "I intend to always be present" or "My life purpose is to stay open to whatever life offers." There are countless variations on this theme. The unintended and unwanted consequence of each of them is an unfortunate passivity toward life. Naming a way of being as your life purpose can rob you of instrumentality and can create an emphasis that runs counter to principled living.

3. Avoid naming a single state of being. Third, and along the same lines, it will probably not pay for you to name as your life purpose one single emotional goal, a goal, say, like happiness or calmness. This is especially true if, as you think the matter through, this turns out not to be your primary goal at all but your secondary one. For example, isn't defending an important principle or engaging in meaningful work a worthier goal than feeling happy? If the way you intend to live requires that you take anxiety-provoking risks, isn't taking those risks your actual goal, and not feeling calm at all times?

4. Avoid adopting too pessimistic a life view. Fourth, it is wise not to create a single life purpose that has built into it an overly pessimistic view of reality or that places safety and survival before all else. It is easy to feel pessimistic, and it is completely rational to want to feel safe and to want to survive. But if you create a life purpose with a conditional quality to it — "Since life is nothing but suffering, I can't wait to leave it" or "Since life is a dangerous affair, my smartest plan is to hide out and play it safe" — then you have chosen a life purpose based on a premise that may be only partially true. When creating your life purposes, double-check your premises as well as your conclusions.

5. Avoid discounting the facts of existence. Fifth, try to choose life purposes that take the facts of existence into account. You can form your life purposes independent of reality, but you can't *live* them independent of reality. Some sense of the interconnection between life purpose and reality needs to be built into the way you name and frame your life purposes. The life purpose phrase that we use in natural psychology, that *our life purpose is to make value-based meaning*, has implied in it the unstated phrase *in the crucible of reality*. If your life purpose doesn't have that phrase built into it, then most likely you will not be ready for the obstacles and indifference that reality is bound to offer.

6. Avoid oversimplified formulations. Sixth, you will want to be careful about not choosing a life purpose that allows you to manifest your values and principles but isn't quite nuanced enough to deal with the fullness of reality. For example, you might contemplate choosing as your life purpose "I intend to live ethically" or "I intend to live authentically." Both of these do a nice job of organizing your life around your values and principles. But they also leave too much out.

For example, what if on a given day you have no particular ethical decisions to make? If you've chosen living ethically as your life purpose, you actually have no life purpose for that day! You may discover that living ethically or living authentically, as beautiful as those phrases are, isn't robust enough to capture certain realities about living, including the realities of our need for easy entertainments, soothing activities, empty diversions, periods that are meaning neutral, and so on.

Choosing Value-Based Meaning-Making

If you guessed that I am leading you somewhere with this, you are right! I would like you to choose "making value-based meaning" as your life purpose. If you choose making value-based meaning, keeping the nuances and subtleties of that phrase in mind, you will enjoy many benefits: You will feel as if you are living your values and your principles. You will see life as a series of opportunities, even if many of them are small, because you will be on the *lookout* for meaning opportunities. You will reduce that portion of your emotional distress caused by meaning crises and existential malaise. And to use a phrase that makes good sense in this context, you will feel as if you are *living authentically.*

Janet Names Her Life Purposes

Let's take a look at the story of Janet, a computer professional from Philadelphia. Janet, like so many people, had fallen into a place of lost meaning and high distress:

> I didn't know what I wanted to do as a young adult, so I wandered around until I found computer programming when I was twenty-six. To me programming was an art. There were few rules about structure. I had artistic freedom to design reports for end users. This adventure continued for many years. During that period, I attended college part-time and eventually earned a degree in data processing management. As computers evolved and moved from the backroom to the forefront of a company's operation, so did computer programming.
>
> As the computer world gained in importance in the business environment, it became a vital strategic tool for companies. Computer programmers had to become more business oriented to survive. Since I spent most of my computer career in corporations, I got to exercise my creativity less and less. Having a family to provide for left me with few options for changing my career to one with greater creative freedom. I felt I had found meaningful work in the first portion of my computer career. However, the feeling of performing meaningful work diminished as time went by. My compensation continued to grow, and I had hoped this would compensate for my growing frustration with my work. Of course it didn't.

Janet grew sad. To the outside world she appeared to be functioning well enough. But she needed medication for stomach problems; she rarely smiled; she spent too much time surfing the Net; she felt critical of her husband and her children; if pressed she would have admitted that life had let her down. She continued putting one foot in front of the other and attending to her responsibilities as her distress mounted. On the verge of some sort of meltdown, she came to see me.

The first thing we discussed was making her job feel meaningful again. Janet expressed that her job could just possibly prove more meaningful if she were allowed more creativity, if she believed more in the service her company provided, and if she were not so tired of having done this work for so long. We examined each of these threads.

She concluded that while she could influence the first by making certain requests and that she could influence the third by taking some time off from work, altering the second felt impossible. This led to a discussion about what sorts of services or products she might feel good supporting. Janet could name some and guessed that there were many others that she didn't know about but that she could certainly research. We had quietly but clearly gotten the subject of changing jobs on the table.

The next thing we discussed was whether there might be some new meaning opportunities for Janet to seize. Usually a client answers this question in the affirmative: most people with meaning problems have been thinking a lot about where they might make some new meaning. Sure enough, Janet had a dream of writing historical nonfiction. She loved reading about the period right after the Second World War and wanted to do a book about the expulsion of indigenous Germans from their central European communities. We talked about adding a morning writing practice to her daily routine.

Next we discussed whether she could alter her evaluation of life as a cheat. It had never occurred to her that she had evaluated it this way. Realizing that she had viewed life so negatively startled her and at the same time made her more hopeful. She realized that if a large part of her distress had to do with nothing more than an evaluation she had made, then perhaps she could change her mind. She wasn't sure that she could "get a grip on her mind," but she agreed that it was a worthy goal. We chatted about what such a change of mind might look and feel like and added that work to her growing list of life purposes.

At times I would interrupt Janet and repeat back to her what she had just said so that she could hear what her formed personality sounded like. Every sentence a person utters is an expression of her formed personality, and of course some utterances are more revealing or important than others. When, for example, Janet remarked, "I probably have no talent for writing nonfiction," that utterance demanded our attention.

I interrupted her and repeated her words back to her, and we chatted about whether such a thought served her. As with all clients, she instantly recognized how much her formed personality, with its characteristically unfriendly self-talk, was going to need upgrading. This became another of her life purposes. I explained the simple technique of hearing a thought, disputing that thought, and substituting more useful language. Janet agreed that practicing such a technique would prove beneficial.

In the end we agreed on several matters — and had a good sense of Janet's newly framed life purposes. She would look for new professional work, seize writing historical nonfiction as a new meaning opportunity, try to evaluate life more positively, and use her available personality to make changes to her formed personality. We added three more having to do with how she would handle recurrent sadness, relate to her children and husband, and lead with calmness. We had made a start.

One huge question remained. Could Janet convince herself to believe in the life purposes she herself had named? People often can't. Those who see life as sad and insufficient, who feel cheated by life and want life to mean something more than it does, maybe something "spiritual" or "more inherently meaningful," typically have a hard time believing in the life purposes that they themselves create.

Their reasoning runs along the following lines: "If all I am doing is nominating this or that as my life purpose, how valid or important is that? That's just me playing a certain kind of game in the face of genuine nothingness, and it is a game that I can see right through. I'd just as soon read a book, have a glass of wine, tend to my roses, or watch a little television than bother with these phony life purposes. Who cares about my life purposes, myself included? Life is too hard and pointless, and my little game of acting like I have some purpose is pretty pathetic."

One narrative will be filled more with irony, another with sadness, a third with anxiety. In essence they all come out the same: if life purpose amounts only to something a person names for herself, something without any cosmic significance, then it amounts to too little or even nothing at all. This is a hangover from the common false belief that life should be meaningful *in some other deeper, more important sense,* that if life isn't meaningful in some cosmic sense, then it is just an empty, burdensome thing.

One of my goals of putting you through boot camp is to help you change your mind about this. I would like you to accept that life matters even though it is exactly this sort of self-created affair. Until you do, you won't feel the quiet satisfaction of making yourself proud, a satisfaction that is available to you once you accept your own life purposes and your own meaning-making abilities. Yes, sometimes you'll see through this operation and be forced to realize that it is "just you" who has created your life purposes. But you can learn to deal with that. You can learn to demand of yourself that you live according to your principles and your values, even if the universe doesn't care one way or the other. You can learn how to effectively respond to the threatening realization that life is a human-sized and not a cosmic-driven enterprise.

I left Janet with this reminder: that now that she had named her life purposes, she would need to believe in them. She would need to believe in them when life pushed back at her, when her job search frustrated her, when anxiety welled up in her, when her first attempts at writing disappointed her. She nodded and claimed to understand. Next would come testing in the crucible of reality.

Naming, Framing, and Living Your Life Purposes

Next I'd like to present a little summary and also a little preview. Here are the steps you can follow in order to name and frame your life purposes — and then start living them:

1. You decide. First, you decide that you and your efforts matter, that you want to live in accordance with your values and principles, and that your life purposes are yours to name and frame. Step 1 involves making a decision and taking a stance.

2. You honor the nature of the task. Next you recognize that naming and framing your life purposes may prove at once complicated and simple. You might create a huge list of the values that matter to you and wonder what on earth to do with such a long and sometimes contradictory list. You might try to factor in all your circumstances, all your principles, and all your personality quirks. How complicated! On the other hand, you might decide that "making value-based meaning" or "doing the next right thing" nicely captures the essence of your life purposes. How simple! You are dealing with a true mouthful, your life and the universe to boot; and yet there may be simple ways of articulating your directions for living beautifully.

3. You make an attempt. You take a stab at naming and framing your life purposes. You might proceed, as Janet did, by looking at various aspects of your life and making certain decisions. This might sound like: "One of my life purposes is to provide myself with meaningful work. A second is to live ethically. A third is to live in love and to create and maintain intimate relationships. A fourth is to show up bravely and really stand up in life."

Maybe this attempt will look like a bulleted list, a menu, a narrative paragraph, or a single sentence or couple of sentences; maybe it will look like two lists, one of long-term life purposes and one of immediate life purposes, or one of "being" purposes and a second of "doing" purposes.

Maybe your attempt will play itself out in a completely different way. There is no one right way to name and frame your life purposes. There is only the attempt to make!

4. You add wrinkles and refinements. In weeks 6 and 7 we'll look at some additional ways of naming and framing your life purposes. We'll look at life purpose statements, at life purpose icons, and at life purpose mantras. Between your first efforts this week and your refinements over the next two weeks, you should acquire a good understanding of your life purposes and of how to "hold" them so that they are readily available to you.

5. You live your life purposes. In week 8 you consolidate your efforts into an announcement of your life purposes, look bravely and forthrightly at how your life purposes can be lived daily, and begin to live them.

6. You appraise your efforts. After boot camp ends, and for the rest of your life, you continue living your life purposes and reworking them as they need updating.

Your Work for the Week

Attempt to name and frame your life purposes. To help you organize your thoughts, you might report to yourself at the end of the week, using the following format:

1. I am holding my life purposes in the following way(s):
2. I think I can translate these life purposes into daily life in the follow way(s):

3. I suspect that the following obstacles may get in the way of my fulfilling my life purposes:

4. Here is my plan for dealing with these obstacles:

We'll continue this work next week. You don't need to arrive at final answers this week. Just make an honorable effort!

Audrey: My Pills and Prescriptions

Audrey, a bookkeeper and watercolorist from Vancouver, described how she responded to the prompts:

I found there were numerous ways I can hold my life purposes:

I will nurture my relationship with my husband, my children, my grandchildren, my extended family, my close friends, and others I meet along the way.

I will work to maintain my health, both physical and mental, through exercise, healthy eating, getting sufficient sleep, and meditative activities.

I will allow myself to do regular creative work and strive to let go of expectations of how that creativity will play itself out.

I will take time to document and enjoy my successes and the things I have done that have made me proud.

I will read and learn new and interesting things about the world around me, including in neuroscience and psychology, and apply what I can to enrich my life and the lives of those I come in contact with.

I will view regular chores such as housework, laundry, and cleaning as a way of providing an appealing environment for myself, as a gift I give myself for my own enjoyment rather than as a burden or an expectation.

I will strive to see the work I do in my home, for our company, and as an artist as work that provides me with an interesting and fulfilling life and as my contribution of my talents and skills to my family, community, and wider world.

I will work to maintain a healthy attitude toward our finances, working to pay off the debt on our house yet still allowing myself to use my/our money to buy things or services that enhance value-based meaning in my/our life.

As to how I can translate these life purposes into daily life, wow, that's a hard one. I think this will require making some sort of chart or poster to put up in my bathroom so that I will look at it every day. If I could get my list of eight items up to twelve, I could apply each one to a month of the year and then work on a specific life purpose each month. Then at the beginning of a new year I can reassess my life purposes and start all over again assigning one to each month.

Another option, if I got my list to twelve items, would be to assign a life purpose to each week and rotate through them every three months. This plan would keep things more interesting and serve as a more regular reminder of all my life purposes.

I suspect that the following obstacles may get in the way of my fulfilling my life purposes. Changing circumstances could certainly affect my life purposes, especially deteriorating health or financial distress due to unforeseen events. I also suspect that I will be tempted to set aside my commitment to my life purposes and slip back into old, more destructive ways of living. I can also see that I will need to understand and deal with the fact that failure is built into this process. There will be days when I will feel like I have failed miserably at living my life purposes and will need to get a grip on my negative self-talk and emotions.

Here is my plan for dealing with obstacles. I see my life purposes as a list of tools I can use to enhance my life and make it feel worthwhile and enjoyable. My life purposes are like a prescription for healthy living. I will need to take certain pills for the rest of my life. When I first started on them, I was really disturbed that I would never be able to return to the days of not taking these pills twice a day. Now, almost six years later, they are as much a part of my life as eating and brushing my teeth.

So I suspect that if I approach my life purposes as a prescription to enrich my life and ensure that I will engage in activities that align with my values, eventually they will become part of the fabric of my life. And when I fall off track, much like getting a medical checkup, I will return to reading about natural psychology and boot camp to remind myself of why I am doing this. In the process I hope that I can be gentle with myself while at the same time holding myself to high standards so that I can be proud of how I am living.

Good luck this week with naming and framing your life purposes. You may find the work difficult, but you will find it immensely valuable!

WEEK 6

Creating Your Life Purpose Statement

Last week you made your first attempt at naming and framing your life purposes. Congratulations on making that effort! This week I want to add to the mix the idea of creating your life purpose statement.

In a way this is easy work: after all, you are only creating a sentence or two. Easiest would be choosing the ones that I suggest: "I am a value-based meaning-maker" and "I do the next right thing." But of course you may well want to create your own; and, if you do, you will be trying to pack that sentence or two with all the information you need. So that may prove to be real work.

It really does pay to have a simple way of remembering your life purposes. As complicated and changeable as your life purposes may prove to be, you will still need to find a way to make them present and available to you in each living moment. One way is to create a life purpose statement that does a succinct but excellent job of reminding you how you intend to live.

A second interesting way to hold your life purposes close is to create a life purpose icon that serves as a visual reminder of them. A third interesting way is to choose a word, sound, or phrase, a life purpose mantra, with the power to do that reminding. We'll look at life purpose icons and mantras next week. This week we will focus on life purpose statements.

Keeping It Simple

Naming your life purposes involves connecting the dots among your desires, your appetites, your dreams, your goals, your values, your principles, your intentions, and everything else pressing down on you and welling up within you. If you were to try to connect all those dots — if, for example, you were to create a document as long as a manual by which to live — you would likely never dip into that manual or find a way to make good use of it. The better choice, and it's a really good one, is to keep it simple.

In one great gulp you take into account the values you want to uphold, the dreams and goals you have for yourself, and the vision you have for comporting yourself in the world, and then you spend whatever time it takes turning that un-wieldy, contradictory material into a coherent statement that reflects your core sentiments.

You might, as a result of your efforts, come up with something like the following: "I will make use of myself every day in the service of truth telling while at the same time getting some real satisfaction out of life through love and work." This is an example of a life purpose statement that, while hardly including every guiding idea of importance that you might add, is nevertheless rich enough to serve.

Naturally yours will be idiosyncratic. Here are some that other folks have created:

Joan, a painter, chose: "I will triumph over the evil that was done to me, which gave me false limitations. I will participate in loving relationships. I will live well and make a meaningful life by working hard to become the best painter I can be, through drawing and painting five or six days a week."

Marcia, a singer-songwriter, trying to manage her mood swings and her stress, riffed on the word *instrument* in her life purpose statement: "My instrument is tuned for the world to move through me. I care for my instrument and keep it tuned. I take care about how I place my instrument in the world."

Pamela: "Action and satisfaction, today and every day."

Sylvia: "I bring my complete self to each moment."

Frank: "I take pride in working with my hands and doing the right thing. I want to die while building a chair, in bed with my wife, or agitating for some cause."

Sonia: "I am at ease in the universe as long as I speak in my voice, appreciate life, and work hard at the things I love."

Lois: "Right here, right now, paying attention and making meaning."

Harrison: "Years of creating a body of work, days of grace and enthusiasm."

Judy: "Passion and presence, courage and conviction."

Melanie: "All contradictions are reconciled if I am for the good."

Jessica, a massage therapist from upstate New York, shared her life purpose statement:

> I created my life purpose statement several years ago, and I still use it: "To manifest the best that I can be: by honoring my wisdom and nurturing my body-mind-spirit; through hearing with inclusiveness and integrity; acting in creative and grace-ful ways; in order to relish the fun and joyful harmony of being. To make my life a playful celebration!"
>
> It took me several months of work to sort out what I truly valued and wanted to focus on. I also constructed it so that I could use the first and last sentences to form a brief powerful statement easy to remember that encompassed the whole mes-sage: "To manifest the best that I can be" and "To make my life a playful celebration!" have become my meaning mantras.
>
> The process of creating this statement really helped me explore not only the bigger things I value but also my daily activities. I was surprised by the true value I found in the small daily actions that I took for granted. Even doing something as simple as serving a meal prepared by the deli began to emerge as an opportunity to find deeper purpose in my life. Instead of thinking I was too busy to cook and would have to pick up something at the store to throw on the table, I began to see this as yet another opportunity to celebrate with play. "How can I present this meal in a way that makes it really pleasant? Can

I have some fun with this?" I don't mean that I started to get loopy by always planning a party. I just started to see my life purpose with the perspective that I wanted, as a playful celebration of life.

Alexis, a documentary filmmaker from Phoenix, described creating her statement as akin to taking a vow:

My efforts at creating a life purpose statement took several attempts over a number of days. Nothing seemed right — and then it came to me very easily. I chose: "To live authentically at all times, to bring empathy and respect to all that I do, to the best of my capability every day. To allow my creative, intuitive self to flourish and to nourish, honor, and cherish my relationship with source every day. To never forget and always allow the freedom of laughter and silliness to weave through my days."

I suspect that this is a work in progress, just as I am, and will change as I move forward. I feel like I am taking a vow. I guess I am, a vow to myself. I feel like I just married myself! Congratulations, me! I know that a life purpose statement of this sort isn't an absolute but just a reminder or guide of the deeper self that I want to see emerging. But I need that reminder. Who doesn't?

Alexander, a chemist from Michigan, reported on how he overcame his initial reluctance:

I had no idea what I was supposed to be doing and balked at the task — and maybe resented it. But the main thing was, I found it intellectually shoddy. Create a single sentence (or even

a paragraph) to encapsulate a life? Come on, now! But something about the exercise kept tugging at me. What resonated
for me was the following odd thought: that sometimes I read a
quote from someone and get the sense that everything I need
is embedded in that quote — that the quote could be lived and
followed. Well, if someone else's words could have that sort of
effect on me, why not my own?

So I played with the exercise with a seriousness — maybe
a self-respect — that I don't usually muster. Finally I came
up with "I own myself." I think I had something in mind like
possessing an owner's manual for the self — that there was
a way to know what to do with myself in every situation, if only
I reminded myself that it was my responsibility to try. I'm sure
that "I own myself" wouldn't work for most people, what with
the word *ownership* being fraught with so much baggage. But I
like it — and I respect it. Does it still stick in my throat to think
that I have a life purpose statement? Yes. Do I find it valuable
nevertheless? Yes, I do!

Lisa, a coach from Milwaukee, described her life purpose
statement as a kind of talisman:

Keeping it simple was the most difficult part of doing this exercise. I tend to like to write a lot of words and to not want to leave
out anything that feels important. Although lots of details and
specifics came to mind, I opted to stay with the essence of what
my life is about. I came up with this: "I am on this earth living
the life as the heroine of my own journey. I choose to live in a
way that supports my values, my authentic self, and my highest
potential. I can do this, and I feel good about the path I am on!"

My statement could probably be shorter, but for now I like it fine. To me it sounds real, and when I say it I feel like I have my feet on the ground and my purpose in place. It's an anchor for me and I need an anchor, since I tend to float into space. What I like about creating a life purpose statement is that by putting it down in written words you create something tangible. It is there to mold, adapt, and share. It becomes a magical talisman — a powerful, magical experience. At least, that's what it's been for me.

Imagine that a dull day is stretching out before you. Instead of engaging in a complex analysis, giving yourself a pep talk to ward off the blues, impulsively opting for a meaning substitute, or standing clueless in the face of a meaning shortfall, you simply say, "Let me invest some meaning." This is similar in form and intent to saying, "Let me do the Christian thing," "Let me do the Stoic thing," or "Let me do the sober thing" and possesses the same utility and power. "I invest meaning daily" could be someone's life purpose statement.

Consider addiction recovery. There are many elements to an addiction recovery program, among them identifying triggers and putting a plan in place for relapse prevention. Each element requires its own particular attention. But the phrase "I am in recovery" works well in and of itself as a constant reminder of your orientation toward sobriety. A phrase like "I make my meaning" or "I make value-based meaning" can stand as a similar reminder of your basic orientation and your moment-by-moment tasks.

In a moment I'll ask you to begin working on your own life purpose statement. But first I'd like you to consider the following twenty quotations. As mentioned by Alexander above, sometimes a quote we read does a superb job of capturing everything we need to know.

Life Purpose Quotations

You may find some useful ideas, phrases, and wordings in the following twenty quotations. I chose them because they all support the idea of making value-based meaning. The first quotation readily turns into the life purpose statement "I am the answer," and so on. If you're moved to do so — and it would be great practice! — you might try transforming each of these twenty quotations into a pithy life purpose statement. Read them for inspiration, and maybe even some guidance.

1. "Life has no meaning. Each of us has meaning and we bring it to life. It is a waste to be asking the question when you are the answer." (Joseph Campbell)
2. "To be yourself in a world that is constantly trying to make you something else is the greatest accomplishment." (Ralph Waldo Emerson)
3. "It is our choices that show what we truly are, far more than our abilities." (J. K. Rowling)
4. "Every choice before you represents the universe inviting you to remember who you are and what you want." (Alan Cohen)
5. "Life isn't about finding yourself. Life is about creating yourself." (George Bernard Shaw)
6. "Life is what we make it, always has been, always will be." (Grandma Moses)
7. "The path to our destination is not always a straight

one. Maybe it doesn't matter which road we embark on. Maybe what matters is that we embark." (Barbara Hall)

8. "The purpose of life is a life of purpose." (Robert Byrne)

9. "Let others lead small lives, but not you. Let others leave their future in someone else's hands, but not you." (Jim Rohn)

10. "Each man must look to himself to teach him the meaning of life. It is not something discovered: it is something molded." (Antoine de Saint-Exupéry)

11. "It's difficult to make people see that what you have been taught counts for nothing, and that the only things worth having are the things you find out for yourself." (Dorothy Sayers)

12. "Life is not discovery of fate; it is continuous creation of future, through choices of thoughts, feelings and actions in the present." (Sanjay Sahay)

13. "If there is a sin against life, it consists perhaps not so much in despairing of life as in hoping for another life and in eluding the implacable grandeur of this life." (Albert Camus)

14. "And at the end of the day, what's more important? Knowing that a few meaningless figures balanced — or knowing that you were the person you wanted to be?" (Sophie Kinsella)

15. "You will have fewer regrets in life if you start focusing and taking responsibility for where you are and where you want to be." (Deborah Day)

16. "Anyone can get a job, but do you have a purpose?" (Tom Butler-Bowdon)
17. "I believe that I am not responsible for the meaningfulness or meaninglessness of life, but that I am responsible for what I do with the life I've got." (Hermann Hesse)
18. "However vast the darkness, we must supply our own light." (Stanley Kubrick)
19. "It isn't death that gives meaning to life. *Life* gives meaning to life. The answer to the meaning of life is hidden right there inside the question." (Wendy Mass)
20. "True happiness is not attained through self-gratification, but through fidelity to a worthy purpose." (Helen Keller)

Your Work for the Week

Please work on creating your own life purpose statement this week. It can be a sentence long, a paragraph long, or something in between. A life purpose statement any longer than a paragraph will probably prove unwieldy. Short is indeed sweet. But this is yours to create. However long or short it is, make it your own!

Work on it until you've come as close as you can in mere words to capturing the essence of your many life purposes. Step back, scratch your head, smile a little at the nature of the task, and then in all seriousness try to grasp the essence of your intentions for your life. Give it a try!

Once you've created your life purpose statement, you

might want to do the following: "translate" those words into a feeling in your body and a message in your brain so that your life purpose intentions become readily available to you. Repeating your life purpose statement over and over is one way to start. Or, to be whimsical about it, you might inscribe it on a banner and hang that banner in your office — or over the inner stage where your thoughts play themselves out. Once you've created your life purpose statement, play with using it!

How do you know if you've created the right life purpose statement? You don't. There is no sure way to know. You create it; you live it; and then you see if it works for you and makes sense to you. Don't balk at this task because you want a guarantee first. Embrace the task, enjoy it, and see what emerges!

At the end of the week try your hand at completing the following three statements:

1. My life purpose statement is:
2. I arrived at it in the following way:
3. I made use of it in the following ways:

Mary: Impossible and Demeaning

Mary, a project manager from Dallas, described the challenge of condensing her life purpose statement:

> Summarizing all the pieces that make my life meaningful so they fit into a sentence or two felt both impossible and demeaning at first. Then, because you had included that list of quotes with the lesson, I was reminded of how often I look to such phrases for inspiration, wisdom, and encouragement.

Nonetheless, I was finding it a challenge to condense my life purpose statement. Ultimately I trusted the process and wound up with two lengthy paragraphs! I continued on. After a few revisions, I came up with something shorter that works for me and that, although my statement doesn't read like poetry and still needs a bit more editing, speaks to me beyond what the words may mean to another: "I choose to live each day taking actions that support me, that keep me connected with others and with the world in a helpful way; that make me feel comfortable in my body as well as joyful, loved, and loving; and that express my creative urges in positive, healthy, life-affirming ways."

Thank you for pushing me to be more deeply thoughtful about how I can make these kinds of profound choices in my daily life. I love boot camp!

Leslie: It Worked Already

Leslie, a writer and community college teacher from San Diego, explained how she condensed a long list into a pithy life purpose statement:

First I made a list of my life purposes:

- Make a contribution through my writing.
- Earn money with my writing.
- Do a better job with my paid work and find a way to make it be part of my contribution.
- Contribute to my community in whatever ways I can, in small practical ways.
- Eat more healthful food.

- Exercise.
- Lose some weight.
- Participate in religious and meditative groups.
- Create an orderly, clean, attractive living space for myself.

It was important to distill all this down to a statement that makes sense, that I can remember, that is flexible, and that is sufficiently nuanced. What I came up with is: "I take care of myself and make a contribution." That's where I've landed.

Actually, a small annoying health issue suddenly became a larger health issue this week. Ordinarily I would have ignored it for a long time. But because of my life purpose statement, I made an appointment with the doctor. Sigh. I don't like going to the doctor. But I feel very proud of myself. My life purpose statement has worked already!

Work this week on creating your life purpose statement. Make as much use as you like of your previous work with creating your menu and mix of meaning opportunities, upgrading your personality, appraising your circumstances, and naming and framing your life purposes. Good luck!

WEEK 7

Creating Your
Life Purpose Icon and Mantra

For the past two weeks you've been working on naming and framing your life purposes. Because of that work you may have landed on your unique way of doing this naming and framing. If that is the case, congratulations! Or you may still be engaged with the process. Either way, we have some new efforts to make this week.

For those of you engaged with the process and still at a bit of a loss, this week may help clarify matters. For those of you who've landed on your way of holding your life purposes, this week's efforts will provide you with some powerful ways of helping to make your life purposes available to you every day.

Your Life Purpose Icon

I want to present the idea of holding your life purposes in a simple way, a way that allows you to live in the light of those purposes without having to continually ask yourself, "What are my life purposes?" or "How should I manifest my life purposes in this set of circumstances?" You do this by creating a life purpose icon either that you physically carry around with you, say on a chain around your neck, or whose image is so clear in your mind that it is always present and serves as your emotional and intellectual anchor. It becomes a filter through which to see the world and a motivator providing you with power and strength in all situations.

As important as it is to be able to describe your life purposes to yourself in words, as in the life purpose statement you worked on last week, it is perhaps even more important that you hold your life purposes in a wordless, intuitive, iconic way. This allows you to meet life's circumstances without having to think about your life purposes or to remind yourself how you intend to be. It frees you to just live.

Think of the way a Christian cross or a Jewish Star of David holds a wealth of meaning. For the religious, those icons carry volumes of information in a simple, portable, brilliant way about what life means and how to live. Other life purpose icons include the clenched fist of black power, the dove of peace, the image of the Buddha, and the rainbow flag of gay rights. These images also provide a wealth of information and meaning for people who hold them as icons.

Countless group icons of this sort exist, including the flags of nations, the iconic saints of orthodox religions, and historical figures of national identity such as Washington and

Lincoln. But rarely does an *individual* create a personal icon that she employs to encapsulate her life purposes and to serve her in this portable, shorthand way.

People tend not to do this because it simply doesn't occur to them. Even if it did, they would still be challenged to accept that they had a right to create a personal icon as weighty as a cross or a Star of David. However, you have not only that right but really the obligation to hold your personal meanings as exactly that important.

It is wonderful to embody in a personal icon your desire to make value-based meaning or any other life purpose you choose. That embodiment is legitimate and useful. Imagine that you could make your life purposes portable by creating your own icon. What would you design or choose? How would you carry it around? Physically, or just in your mind's eye?

Paula, a painter from Oregon, told me about her walking stick:

My life purpose icon is the walking stick. I selected it because I find that it perfectly represents my journey through life. I do have a walking stick in real life and I treasure it. It is somewhat crooked, as is the path of life. But it is sturdy and I cannot break it. It is a light and dark stick, representing the duality of life — day and night, stormy and peaceful, happy and full of strife. It is everything that life is and is not. And it was born from something rooted to this earth, just as I am.

My walking stick icon is a great comfort to me when I feel afraid or lost. It supports me when I feel weak and protects me when I feel scared. Probably in creating it I was thinking about the phrase "Thy rod and thy staff, they comfort me," from Psalm 23, but now it has taken on a completely personal meaning. I don't at all regret not having a lot of material or monetary wealth, for I realized long ago that those things are not what bring me satisfaction and peace at the end of the day. Instead I just keep painting — and walking, accompanied by my walking stick.

Greg, a geologist from Montana, chose an image of an object instead of the object itself:

I'm a rock kind of guy and so of course when I first thought about the idea of life purpose icons, many versions of rocks came to mind, including fossilized rocks and their connection to life, sedimentary rocks with their ideas of regularity and layering, gemstones with their sheer beauty and iconic resonances, and so on. Each of these made sense. But I began to realize that I was putting the cart before the horse by thinking about icons before I'd really considered what my life purposes *were*.

So that's what I did. I sat down and tried to figure that out. And finally I had to agree that I both understood and liked the idea of making meaning as my life purpose. It took me a little while to get a picture of what that actually meant, but at some point I got how the phrase *making value-based meaning* painted a pretty darn good picture of my intentions.

However, no icon came to mind. Even though I like the phrase, it doesn't really conjure up an image and certainly not an image connected to rocks! But then one day it struck me. I didn't need a literal representation, just a personal association. And since I've always loved stones from streams, I found a particularly beautiful small smooth stone in the riverbed near our house, I really looked at it, and I imprinted its beauty into my brain. I can't put into words what my icon looks like — but being able to describe it must be secondary. All that matters is whether or not I can see it — and I can!

Sandra, a sculptor from Maine, explained why she chose a lighthouse as her icon:

My personal icon is a lighthouse. First of all, a lighthouse is steadfast. To pursue my art, I have to be persistent and work consistently. I have to be dedicated to doing something every day to get the word out about my work and to practice my art. A lighthouse also stands out and stands alone. It is important to me that my ideas are singular and not derivative. In order for me to be original, like it or not, I must stand up. And a lighthouse also has its own beauty and strength. It's built to withstand the worst storms, it's a fantastic design with a tremendously useful function, and it's a genuinely positive image. If my art could be that powerful, I would be truly fulfilling my life purpose.

A walking stick, a polished stone, a lighthouse — what will your life purpose icon be? Please give that some thought right now, or carve out some time this week to do this work. You might start by reviewing your efforts from the past two weeks so that you have a clear picture of how you are naming and framing your life purposes in words. Or you might go directly to imagery, either looking in your mind's eye, in nature, on the Internet, in books, or in whatever way comes

up for you. You are looking for a powerful, personal, visual
representation of your life purposes, one that works as deeply
and simply as a cross, a star, or a flag.

The second step, once you've landed on your life purpose
icon and feel confident that it's the right one for you, is to
think through how you will employ it. Will you go to a jewelry maker and have it fabricated? Will you create a screen-
saver with it as the motif? Will you draw a picture of it and
carry it in your wallet? Will you keep it in your mind's eye
only? Try to complete this two-step process of landing on a
life purpose icon and making that life purpose icon available
to you in some intimate, permanent way.

Your Life Purpose Mantra

There's no reason why your life purposes can't be associated with and captured by a sound, a word, or the shortest
of phrases: by the sound of wind chimes, by some notes of
music, by a single musical note, by a bird's song, by a sound
like *om*, by a word like *courage*, or by a phrase like *be here now*.

A sound might work for you. The world is full of mourn-
ful sounds, evocative sounds, beautiful sounds, memorable
sounds, sounds of all sorts: train whistles, the sound of a
screen door closing, the sound of a baby laughing. If some
sound holds particular meaning for you or has the power
to remind you of your life purposes, then that sound is vital
to you!

How might you employ it? If it's a string of notes and you
can play an instrument, create a daily ritual and play yourself
your life purpose music. If you can't play an instrument, have

a musical friend record your life purpose music so that you can ceremonially play it for yourself daily or several times a day. You can record any sound and make the time to listen to your audio mantra. Or you can carry it around in your own mind, just the way we carry snatches of songs, and listen to it "inside" in a regular, mindful way.

What about using a word or short phrase (shorter than your life purpose statement) as a mantra? A mantra is usually associated with praying or meditating, but its core definition is "a word or phrase repeated often to express one's basic beliefs." Think of resonant words such as *courage, authenticity, rebel, truth teller,* or *meaning-maker.* Each such word can carry a world of information and feeling. If shamanism holds power for you, then the name of your power animal — jaguar, crow, cougar, lynx, eagle — might be such a word. Maybe a place word carries power for you: *Paris, fjord, desert,* or *valley.* Maybe it's a word like *life, love,* or *liberty.* For me the word that carries the most meaning is *process,* a word that might work for virtually no one else!

Here are three examples of mantras from boot campers:

1. I decided on "the Breath of Life" as my mantra. I choose it because it reminds me to breathe deeply when there's tension or anxiety and to breathe deeply simply for health and vitality. When my focus starts with my breath, it centers and grounds me, and I feel more inner directed rather than scattered with tasks or activities. It also allows me the space to stay in tune with the bigger perspective of my life.

2. For my mantra I chose "Embrace the integrity of what is." I chose that short phrase because it encompasses

what I see myself doing as a woman and as an artist. It puts me squarely in the truth of the moment and reflects what I believe is so important: to actively accept what is in all its integrity. It reminds me that it is not my will that creates the moment but a much larger design for life of which I am a small but vital part.

3. I chose "I am the light of my own life." Light has many qualities that I want to bring into my life. It is creative, transformative and healing. From a metaphorical perspective, I have clearer vision and fresh insight when I see the light. I need a certain light to work in and to be productive, and the right light also positively affects my mood and emotions. My mantra helps me to think that I carry the optimal light within, so I don't need to seek it from a source other than myself.

Anything can remind you that you have ideals and purposes: a musical tone, a shaft of light, a single word, a short phrase, even a certain smile that you decide to wear. No doubt people would find it strange if before each decision you made you hummed a middle C, incanted "jaguar," or smiled a certain smile. But we mustn't be the least bit concerned about the stares of strangers! If you discover that a mantra of this sort serves you, please don't avoid using it out of self-consciousness.

Using Your Name as a Mantra

Potentially the most useful and powerful mantra is your own name. What word or sound does a better job of carrying your life purposes, your identity, and your intentions? Wouldn't it be wonderful to have your name do this work? However, if "Dan" or "Andrea" conjures only your anxieties, your short-comings, or your regrets, then "Dan" or "Andrea" will hardly work as your life purpose mantra. On the other hand, if you follow up on the work of week 3, in which you began upgrading your personality by becoming the person who makes herself proud by her efforts, then your name might receive an equal upgrade.

People have remarkably variable and typically very strong reactions, both negative and positive, to using their name as their life purpose mantra. Aneesah, a painter from the Netherlands, reported on how she turned her name into an acronym:

> I have had some bad experiences with my name. It is Persian and means "the affectionate one." I used to be proud of this until people took advantage of my innocence and generous nature and my family expected me to put up with abuse and to give into a bullying sibling by being "the affectionate one."
>
> The narcissist I married started using my family pet name, the short form of my name, Anee, to feign intimacy and to manipulate me. Other times he would bring a tone of exasperation when using my name so as to intimidate me into not asking questions. Finally I stood up for myself and announced that I would not tolerate having my name used in that way, and he got the message. I am slowly making peace with my name and I have been considering using it as my life purpose mantra.
>
> This week I started playing with my name as an acronym to start bringing some positive feelings into it and to have my

name stand for what *I* want it to stand for. Every day I worked on using my name in ways that upgrade my personality and help me heal all those "meaning leaks" around my name. I played with each letter and expanded my first ideas into incantations and affirmations. I came up with the following:

A = I **a**waken to freedom.
N = I **n**ominate myself to make meaning.
E= I am **e**xceptional and prove the exception.
E = I **e**mbrace this moment.
S = I **s**tep into a resourceful state.
A = **A**ppreciation rules!
H = I return **h**ome to self-compassion, and strength.

I believe that my name, when used in this way, will help me focus on what's meaningful, serve to reduce my anxiety, and bring me more contentment. Sometimes I'll focus on the letters in order, and other times I'll focus on just one letter and make a kind of game of it. Today I also noticed the following: that my name has seven letters, which is particularly useful, since my life purpose icon has seven segments, each of which stands for a particular stage of my journey. So I am discovering new, resourceful, and enriching ways to make use of what I am learning!

Kimberly, a singer-songwriter from Nashville, explained how she combined using her name and her icon:

I had chosen a rocket as my life purpose icon. My favorite fantasy is to see the Earth from space. I want to build meaning in my life by living and helping others to live in the whole world, to explore beyond everyday limits, to reach what's just out of sight. I chose the rocket to remind me of my purpose because, just as ships are built to sail the seas rather than to languish in harbors, rockets are built to blast off rather than to stand on the launchpad. Mistakes will be made, postponements and problems will arise, but persistence pays off when we blaze into the unknown.

I put a rocket charm on my key ring and a large picture of the Mars *Explorer* rocket on my wall chart. Both remind me — sometimes rather unexpectedly during the day — that I am built for breaking boundaries, both those of inner space and those of outer space. Not everyone will understand. Not every friend will cheer me on or go with me. But I will meet other pilots who share my enthusiasm for an expanding consciousness and a meaningful mission. Oh, by the way, I named my rocket charm the *Kimberly*.

So it makes perfect sense to me to use "Kimberly" as my life purpose mantra. I can tell that using my name as an incantation will help to calm and also to excite me; it will prompt me to forgive myself and to hold myself accountable; and it will push me to explore or to build boundaries as needed. The *Kimberly* stands for my available personality, for that person who can love, support, nurture, guide, protect, and remind me that my purpose is to make meaning in this life.

Your Work for the Week

Your work for the week is the following:

1. Identify and/or create your life purpose icon.
2. Picture how you will add it to your life.
3. Add it!

4. Identify and/or create your life purpose mantra.
5. Picture how you will add it to your life.
6. Add it!
7. Think through whether using your name as your life purpose mantra makes sense for you.
8. If it does, begin to use it!

Lara: White Trumpeter Swan Feather

Lara, a lawyer and birder from Wisconsin, explained how she chose both her icon and her mantra:

> I chose as my life purpose icon a white trumpeter swan feather. I chose the swan feather because of the amazing experience I had with some swans this summer. Trumpeter swans are not common in our area since they usually nest farther north. But this summer we saw that four trumpeter swans had stayed the summer at the lake where we have a summer property.
>
> Later in the season, while canoeing up the river that feeds into the lake, we came upon the four swans and what looked like a nest. One of the swans was obviously molting, and there were quite a few large flight feathers both on the nest and in the water. We managed to collect a few of the feathers after the birds had flown to a safer area on the river. On another occasion we found ourselves canoeing beside a young swan and got some great pictures. This was a significant event and not one easily repeated, so I feel that the feather represents something very special in my life.
>
> To me the trumpeter swan feather is a symbol of beauty and freedom. I have been a birder for at least twenty-five years,

and it is an important part of who I am. I have also recently decided to concentrate on learning to paint birds as part of my creative work. This particular feather is a fine representation of that part of my life. It reminds me to take things more lightly, since I have a tendency to be quite serious.

Its white color reminds me to choose to uphold my highest values. The fact that it's a molted feather reminds me that life is always changing but that life goes on. The feather is a flight feather, so it reminds me that I can have lofty goals and still do important things in my life. It is a useful feather and I can be useful too, even as I grow older. The feather is constructed so that even if the sections of it become separated, when it is preened or just stroked, the feather knits back together. This represents resilience to me.

As to my life purpose mantra, I chose "I am flourishing." In positive psychology five elements are considered important: positive emotions, engagement, meaning/purpose, achievement, and relationships. As I live my life purpose I believe that I can continually work on these five elements, and in doing so I can indeed flourish. It is interesting that another meaning of the word *flourish* is "an ornamental trumpet call." It ends up working well with my icon of the trumpeter swan feather!

This mantra reminds me that no matter what is happening in my life, I can still flourish. Often my biggest struggle is with my emotions, which are not always so positive. By considering all five of the elements, I can take a more holistic view of my life and see that to flourish also means to have good relationships and to have meaning and purpose and to accomplish goals. It means to be engaged in my life and the things that I do. By using my mantra regularly I remind myself that I am indeed flourishing. I would like to use this mantra in meditation as well as have it posted in my studio.

As to using my name as my life purpose mantra, I don't think that would work for me, although I'm not sure why. I have never really liked my name, although I love the aunt I was named after. I am thinking that I only use my name to myself when I am down on myself, as in, "So, Lara, why did you do *that?*" Maybe this indicates my deep lack of confidence and my inability to appreciate my own strengths. More thinking is needed on this!

Janine: Brilliant Orange Pumpkin

Janine, a consultant and entrepreneur from Michigan, talked about the color of joy:

I chose a brilliant orange pumpkin as my life purpose icon. I thought about all the icons that have had meaning for me in the past and tried to make them fit. Nothing felt right and nothing new was coming. The next day while I was walking to work, the image of a huge orange pumpkin came into my mind, and that fit perfectly.

I love pumpkins, whether for eating or just for keeping around for the winter as friends. A pumpkin is orange, and for me that is the color of joy. A pumpkin is also a vehicle for magic and transformation. Cinderella rides to the ball in a pumpkin, and so I will ride deeper and deeper into my life purpose in a pumpkin carriage, sans prince. Pumpkins also have a tremendous amount of seeds. Planting seeds of joy is what I'm up to. By the time I got to work I thought, well, maybe that's not the right icon, maybe it should be something just a bit loftier, although nothing new or better replaced the pumpkin.

That night I had a dream that someone gave me a gift. I couldn't see the person handing me the beautifully wrapped little box. When I finally got to the center of the tissue paper, I was holding in my right hand a beautiful ceramic pumpkin about two inches in diameter with gold inlay. Then I awoke and laughed. The pumpkin is the perfect icon for me. I love their strength, the way they're bursting with ideas (seeds), their endurance, and the way they take their place in the world, which I believe is what we are all being asked to do. And really, they create so much with so little!

As to my life purpose mantra, I chose my name. A lot of beautiful words hold meaning for me, and I've used them in the past as mantras or as words to meditate on. I wanted to push myself a bit further and decided to use my name as my life purpose mantra. My name means "gift from God." It has taken my entire life to get to a place where people who know me would say that I am living up to, or into, my name. I feel like my life is a gift from God (God in the broadest sense). It's also time to claim my own gifts, and like the pumpkin, I contain all the seeds I need for creating passion, joy, magic, and transformation for myself and for others. It feels like a powerful way to claim what is.

I hope that you'll flat-out enjoy this week's work of creating your life purpose icon and mantra. If you do the work, try to go all the way and incorporate your icon and your mantra into your daily life.

WEEK 8

Living Your Life Purposes

This week is about practicing living your life purposes. If you've done the work leading up to this week, you've gained a lot of insight and probably have a very good sense of how to name, frame, and hold your life purposes. However, you also know that life is not set up to make living your life purposes easy. Your circumstances conspire against you; your formed personality conspires against you; your not being in the habit of leading with your life purposes conspires against you. In other words, living your life purposes is an adventure and a project!

No hurricane gathering off the coast cares anything about your life purposes. No CEO deciding to fire you and five thousand of your fellow employees cares anything about your life purposes. No muse sitting on some rooftop exists to help you write your novel, and no army of advocates stands in waiting to market it. You may have an excellent, even a perfect, sense of your life purposes, but life is prepared to throw you one monkey wrench after another. Calmly accept that you must live your life purposes in the crucible of reality and that your work doesn't end when this boot camp ends.

Learn to appreciate how much your circumstances matter. If you don't appreciate the power of circumstance to reduce your experiences of meaning, you'll slowly but surely begin to cross meaning opportunities off your menu. Take the following simple example. You have a good sense of what brings you joy, let's say watching a baseball game in the warm afternoon sun. You go to a game, but your arthritis flares up and you can't enjoy yourself. You could say to yourself either of the following: "I don't enjoy baseball anymore" or "My current circumstances are preventing me from enjoying baseball." Saying the former is an accidental renunciation and begins to wipe baseball off your menu of joyful opportunities. Saying the latter, acknowledging your circumstances and placing the problem at the feet of your circumstances, allows baseball to remain on your menu of joyful opportunities.

You may not enjoy building your business, but that doesn't mean that building a business is no longer a meaning opportunity. You may not have loved or admired any of your recent intimate partners, but that doesn't mean that relating is no longer a meaning opportunity. You may have hit a dead end in your science career and find yourself trapped in a numbing area of research, but that doesn't mean that science is no longer a meaning opportunity. You do not have to discard building a useful business, enjoying intimate relationships, or doing interesting science as a life purpose. What you do have to do is *deal with your circumstances.*

Living your life purposes involves much more than putting one foot in front of the other and occasionally reminding yourself of your purposes. It means making the necessary changes so that you are actually *living* your life purposes. The phrases that I'm promoting, *making value-based meaning* and *doing the next right thing*, each have embedded in them the idea that you are bound up in a dance with reality, including the reality of your formed personality, your habits of mind, your previous and current choices, your circumstances, and everything else life can throw at you. Doing the next right thing may mean dealing with any one of these natural impediments.

If you decide that the next right thing is to practice calmness, but life is making you highly anxious, it will not be easy to practice calmness. If you decide that the next right thing is to spend two hours working on your suite of paintings but you feel listless and uninspired, it will not be easy to spend two hours working on your suite of paintings. Yet practicing calmness and working on your suite of paintings are still the next right things to do. You are obliged to make your value-based meaning in the face of — even in the teeth of — these sorts of difficulties. Boot camp didn't really make life easier! But I hope it has alerted you to your tasks and painted a picture of what a life of meaning and purpose can look like.

On the other hand, many moments will prove blissfully easy — and maybe much easier than before — now that you are getting the hang of making meaning and living your life purposes. On some days you'll make yourself extremely proud by your efforts and, feeling proud, find your next challenges easier to tackle. Maybe for a whole series of moments, hour after hour and day after day, you'll feel that life is meaningful and that you are living your life purposes beautifully. All that may also happen. There will be pratfalls, life insults, failures, unwanted pounds, setbacks, and who knows what else, but there will also be ease, happiness — and results.

Employing the Boot Camp Metaphor

I want to briefly return to the metaphor of military boot camp to remind you of the tasks associated with living your life purposes. So fall in, and here goes:

1. Things change immediately when you enter the military, just as they change when you go from living in an ordinary way one day and deciding to live as a meaning-maker the next. That change is exactly as radical a change as enlisting, if you let it be. Before boot camp you were "just living," and now you are trying to live in the light of your life purposes. Boot camp is an opportunity for dramatic change.

2. Military basic training continually tests you, and it is made clear that you are *being* tested. Life will test you too. Whether or not any of us wants to frankly acknowledge it, life is a testing ground.

By acknowledging this truth, you stand up a little straighter and are more likely to lead with your life purposes. Boot camp is an opportunity to accept that life will test you.

3.   In military boot camp the first thing you do every day is "fall in." Rather than standing at attention, as you do in the army, you might start your day by paying attention. You wake up, consider your day, and make mindful decisions about how you intend to live your life purposes, what meaning investments you intend to make, and what meaning opportunities you intend to seize. By starting your day with a morning meaning check-in, you remind yourself of and focus on your life purposes.

4.   In military boot camp you're taught to seize opportunities and to act quickly since your life may depend on it. If you see your life as a project and you as the project manager, you will want to be a very quick-witted and quick-acting project manager. Each day act bravely, quickly, and powerfully in the service of your life purposes.

5.   Drill is an integral part of basic training. It is akin to the boring, repetitive aspects of life that we must maturely accept. But just as a drill team can turn ordinary drill into something beautiful, you can turn repetitive acts into the beauty of a life lived intentionally. Repeat those activities that serve your life purposes, and learn to excel at them.

6.   At boot camp regular inspections are conducted. If

we intend to think and act in accordance with our life purposes, we have to monitor ourselves to make sure that we are doing precisely that. The word *inspection* nicely captures the flavor of that self-monitoring process. Make sure to inspect your thoughts and actions to ensure that they are aligned with your life purposes.

7. Military boot camp pushes you beyond your comfort zone, and so does life purpose boot camp, which helps us tap into reserves we don't even know we possess. Of course we don't want to access those reserves by yelling at ourselves like some internal sadistic drill sergeant, but we do want to know that we possess them. If the vagaries of life or the pursuit of one of your life purposes stretches you, remember that you possess real reserves for tapping into.

Basic training doesn't turn a raw recruit into an accomplished soldier. After basic training you proceed to further training, either in some specialty like radio operation or tank repair or on to advanced infantry training. If in the army's wisdom you are to remain a foot soldier — a grunt — then advanced infantry training is your next challenge.

In advanced infantry training you learn to use new, more powerful weapons and engage in harder tasks, like negotiating the night escape, learning evasion, and taking survival courses. You continue learning, you continue feeling anxiety, and you continue improving, and you also make new mistakes and encounter other features of your formed personality. Let's embrace this exact change: the movement from boot camp to active duty!

Organizing Your Efforts

The first step in living your life purposes is making sense of the work you've done over the past several weeks and deciding how you're going to hold your life purposes in awareness every day.

If you primarily intend to use your life purpose statement, how exactly will you use it? If you're attracted to the idea of using your life purpose icon or your life purpose mantra, how will you employ them so that they inform your life? How will you keep your life purposes fresh and available to you as you go about your days? You might try some or several of the following techniques:

1. Name a single focus for the week. This might sound like:

- This week I am staying calm.
- This week I am looking for meaningful work.
- This week I am minding my health.
- This week I am working on my novel every day.
- This week I am leading with compassion.

2. Name a weekly way of being and also a weekly concrete doing. This might sound like:

- This week I am staying calm and working on my novel.
- This week I am practicing patience and looking for a new job.
- This week I am risking humiliation and joining the dating scene.
- This week I am managing my anxiety and having that hard conversation with Bill.
- This week I am staying open to joy and visiting the new show at the museum.

3. Name a series of two or more action goals. This might sound like:

- This week I am building my home business and getting a grip on my finances.
- This week I am working on my novel and submitting my completed manuscript to agents.
- This week I am renewing old acquaintances by reaching out to Tom, Dick, Jane, and Harry.
- This week I am upgrading my personality in three ways: by focusing on recovery, by starting my exercise program, and by reducing the amount of Internet surfing I do.
- This week I am making two new meaning investments, first in my long-term plan to relocate and second in learning the technology I need to know to move my business forward.

4. Name an overarching life purpose for the week. This might sound like:

- This week I am doing one right thing after another.
- This week I am being my best self.
- This week I am making value-based meaning.
- This week I am making some new meaning investments.
- This week I am seizing some new meaning opportunities.

5. Plan for the long term. This might sound like:

- This week I am painting a picture of the life I want to be leading next year.

- This week I am taking stock of the creative work I've done so far and opening up to the question, "What sort of creative work do I want to do next?"
- This week I am having a conversation with myself about what it means to maybe have fifty years of living left.
- This week I am starting to get rid of the baggage that prevents me from thinking clearly about the future.
- This week I am creating a clear, simple, powerful two-year plan for myself.

6. Use your life purpose statement. You might:

- Print it out and wear it as a wristband.
- Add it to the signature line on your email.
- Record it and listen to it.
- Remind yourself of it before meals or in some other routine way.
- Turn it into a poster that you post on the wall.

7. Use your life purpose icon. You might:

- Have it made into a piece of jewelry.
- Have it made into a sculpture for your desk.
- Draw it roughly and put it up on the wall.
- Enlist an artist to draw it or paint it.
- Be with it in your mind's eye several times a day.

8. Use your life purpose mantra. You might:

- Say it as you begin each of your daily meaning investments.
- Record it and listen to it.
- Incorporate it into your morning meaning check-in.

- Incant it when anxiety wells up in you.
- Incant it whenever you need a reminder of your intentions.

9. *Create a morning check-in ritual.* You might:

- Engage in a morning meaning check-in and identify the meaning investments you intend to make and the meaning opportunities you intend to seize.
- Engage in a morning life purpose check-in in which you consciously align your day with your life purposes.
- Read your life purpose statement.
- Spend time with your life purpose icon.
- Repeat your life purpose mantra.

10. *Give yourself a thinking prompt before you go to sleep.* This might sound like:

- "I wonder how I might live my life purposes tomorrow?"
- "I wonder what new meaning investment I might make tomorrow?"
- "I wonder what new meaning opportunity I might seize tomorrow?"
- "I wonder if my life purposes need any updating?"
- "I wonder what I will bring to tomorrow?"

How would you like to approach living your life purposes this week? Take some time to think this through.

Seven Tips for Living Your Life Purposes

Living your life purposes is an elegant dance in which you make concerted efforts and also relax and enjoy; you accept yourself and also upgrade yourself; and you plan, dream, and hope and also detach from outcomes. You pencil in effort and you pencil in ease. You smile at your quirky thoughts, and you also dispute the thoughts that don't serve you. Perfection isn't the goal — but you can definitely get good at this!

You can get good at understanding, creating, and repairing meaning. If you slip off your path, you can return to it by repeating your life purpose mantra or by meditating on your life purpose icon. When you not only choose your life purposes but, more fundamentally, also choose to *have* life purposes, the desire to pat yourself on the back will well up in you. You deserve that pat on the back! Let's take a moment and summarize by looking at the step-by-step process of living your life purposes.

1. Name and frame your life purposes. First you will need to name them and frame them in the ways we've been discussing throughout boot camp. Whether you adopt the life purpose I suggest, "My life purpose is to make value-based meaning," or whether you adopt some other life purposes, you will need to know in some clear, memorable way what your intentions are for your life.

2. Put your life purposes into action. Your life purpose statement is likely to be both powerful and abstract. If you intend to make value-based meaning you still need to know what meaning investments you intend to make and what meaning opportunities you intend to seize. You need to know not only that you are writing a novel but also what novel you are writing. You need to know not only that you intend to save for a rainy day but also how much of your paycheck you are putting away weekly. Living your life purposes requires this kind of concreteness and exactness.

3. Orient yourself daily and consistently toward your life purposes. Starting the day by reading the newspaper or visiting your usual Internet sites is different from starting it by reminding yourself of your life purposes and deciding how to manifest them. Your life purposes will only become your guiding forces if you consistently orient yourself in their direction.

4. Upgrade your personality. Look in the mirror. Transform yourself into the person equal to living the life purposes you've named. If your life purposes require assertiveness, courage, and resilience, then you need to manifest assertiveness, courage, and resilience. Upgrading your personality and keeping track of who you need to be is ongoing work. Indeed, upgrading your personality *is* one of your life purposes. The idea of making value-based meaning includes the idea that you will be making ongoing meaning investments in *you*.

5. Apply your principles every day, and engage in tactics that support your life purposes. Every day that you say to yourself, "I'll begin tomorrow" is a sad, lost day. Start your day with a morning meaning check-in or some other practice that reminds you that you intend to live your life purposes. Even if your morning check-in is just a reminder that you mean to be a certain way — sober, open, present, compassionate — that small reminder is still valuable.

6. Monitor your efforts. Living provides you with new circumstances, new experiences, and new information that you can then use to update your plans and methods. Your life purpose may not change an iota, you may still stand behind making value-based meaning, but how you manifest your life purpose is bound to change as doors close and doors open. Take stock regularly.

7. *Take special notice of big changes.* Are you the same person in the same set of circumstances with the same life purposes if you have children, if you begin to doubt the rightness of your career, if you've spent thirty years doing the same sort of work, if your nation is invaded, if you lose your lifelong mate? Check in with yourself regularly but especially when some large change has occurred.

Your Work for the Week

Your work for the week is to live your life purposes. Stay focused on keeping them front and center. At the end of the week you may want to organize your thoughts in the following way:

1. I used the following device to hold my life purposes (my life purpose statement, my life purpose icon, my life purpose mantra, or something else):
2. I tried to remind myself of and keep focused on my life purposes throughout the week in the following way(s):
3. Living my life purposes went as follows:

Elaine: I Lost My Way — or Did I?

Elaine, a painter and coach from Toronto, described how she redefined making meaning:

Sitting down now to contemplate this week, my first thought is that I lost my way.

This boot camp has been a big part of my life over the past eight weeks, but somehow this week I got off track. I've had some health issues to deal with and some news about a gallery that I haven't wanted to face. There was also news of a new grandbaby on the way, a daughter setting the date for her wedding, and preparations for a weekend getaway. Nothing big, nothing life changing, just regular life, but still I found myself running from activity to activity, completely ignoring my life purpose.

Or did I?

On the day that I needed to deal with the gallery I also helped a friend commit to returning to her coaching practice in January. "I choose to remember that every day brings both joys and challenges."

When I went in for a medical test I eased my anxiety by purposely looking around and feeling grateful for this facility available to me through our amazing Canadian health-care system. "I will feel better if I embrace gratitude."

Shopping for our large family — our immediate family numbers fifteen — on a limited budget takes a certain amount of attention and energy. I *love* Christmas shopping! "Through my actions I can use my strengths and talents to create a rich and fulfilling life for myself and those I love and care for."

I got the results of some blood tests back and decided that it was important for my health to lose a little weight. So I have been researching how I might go about doing that, including making an appointment with a dietitian. It is important to me to be healthy and feel good, so I want to invest the time and energy into working on this aspect of my life. A lot of my week was taken up doing this, shopping for food, deciding on menus, and so on. All this I consider value-based meaning-making, and I have invested in it every day this week.

It was a busy week and I frequently asked myself, "What is the next right thing to do?" This helped to keep me on track and focused. Although I was less mindful of my life purpose than I would have liked to be, I think I actually structured my week around my life purposes after all!

Lois: Relaxing into Myself

Lois, a publicist from Maryland, mused on the importance of lightening up:

This week I applied my life purpose statement, icon, and mantra to the task of lightening up on my work efforts and focusing on one of my life purposes, namely, being in an easy space of relaxing activities.

It was a vacation week, and I wanted to see how much I had changed, since one of my original goals was to lighten up, be kinder to myself, and mindfully apply relaxation techniques in my life. Given that this was my first time using these tools and techniques over a five-day period with any specific focus, I learned that although some parts were easy, at other times I felt challenged and fell back on old habits.

Important goals were self-kindness and self-compassion. I also wanted to allow myself to "just be" during these five days. I made a conscious decision to give myself this time and apply the boot camp tools to this aspect of my life. I used breathing and pausing as my major methods. When I set my intent strongly it worked better than when I was more casual about it. It also made me stronger when I thought of the sequoia tree that I had selected as my icon.

Relaxing is getting easier, and I can see more self-kindness and self-compassion starting to unfold. As they unfold, I am becoming painfully aware of how hard I can be on myself. One of the benefits I started to see was not jumping so quickly from one thing to the next. It became more of an easing. I think being aware of this is a good lesson for me. I'll be able to use the boot camp tools to relax into myself and also apply them beneficially to other areas of my life.

Louise: *Today* Is an Inch-Wide Pink Bar

Louise, a freelance writer from Tacoma, talked about the importance of focus and energy:

I've been wearing some of my icons, special pieces of jewelry. My iconic beads sit here on my computer waiting for me to find time to string them into usable rosary beads. The stones reflect layered light in subtle flashes, tiny hidden worlds. I've been practicing my mantra, which is simply "Earth/stars; reach out/ connect," paired with conscious breathing. That does it for me.

If I'm out walking, especially walking in my labyrinth, as I do most evenings, I might add some details to the chant, and a visualization of a golden web. I particularly like the combo: the prayer, the breath, the walking meditation, the beads, the image held in my mind, being out in nature watching the sky deepen, hearing the owls wake up. The routine reduces my anxiety and energizes me while keeping me focused.

Focus and energy are the keys. I don't think lack of meaning is really my issue. The world blossoms with innate meaning for me. It's more alignment with and connection to the meaning. My problem is more that I'm swamped with all the work I've taken on. My hopes and efforts are ambitious, even though I'm a solo act with few resources. The sense of being continually overwhelmed is disheartening. I can feel defeated before I start just by the number and weight of urgent matters.

Inspired by one of the earlier boot camp lessons, I've split the overwhelming avalanche of my to-do list into two separate sticky notes. One is labeled *Big Picture,* which is a list of everything. The other is just [*Today's Date*] — a daily way to focus. I can select a small bit of something urgent from the *Big Picture* and put it on the *Today* plan, along with simple repetitive items like "wash dishes." No longer are these my to-do lists; now each is a *Menu of Choices and Opportunities.*

To make the menus appetizing, I've made them colorful, with short reminders: "Align actions with intentions and values," "Seek nutritional mix," "Do next right thing," and "Today I invest my energy, time, and creativity in this." Then there are menu categories — "paid work," "chores," "self-care," and more — with a jot about the values served by the category. For instance, "paid work" is really "core survival," while "chores" has the reminder "enhance daily livability." Now I add and subtract action items daily.

Today is an inch-wide pink bar that lives on the far right of my computer screen, so I am reminded to check in with myself throughout the day. True to form, I can't get through half the *Today* list on most days. That's okay; I don't really expect to. It's a menu. I can look and see what's the "next right thing." The method is helping me stay focused on small pieces that I can chew without choking!

The simple goal for this week is to begin to live your life purposes. Boot camp has provided you with many strategies for doing that, and now it is time to put those into practice.

Your Final Report

When you complete basic training you go on a short leave, and then you report to your next duty station, where you learn to fix radios, fire mortars, maintain tanks, and so on. There is no taking stock after basic training. You aren't asked to write an essay about your experiences. You don't gather in a circle to express your feelings about boot camp. You pack your gear, get on a bus, and go home.

With life purpose boot camp, however, you have the opportunity to take stock. What follow are four final reports from life purpose boot campers. I think you'll find them interesting and enjoyable. Read them, and then buckle down to the task of processing your own boot camp experiences through writing a final report. Feel free to create your own report any way you like. I suggested the following format to boot campers, and this is the format they used:

1. What I learned:
2. What I accomplished:
3. How it helped me:
4. What I would like to focus on going forward:

If you haven't managed to go through boot camp yet, these reports may inspire you to begin.

June: The Tumult of Accidents and Obstacles

June, a corporate executive and fledgling writer from Tampa, shared her final report:

1. What I learned: Most important was the emphasis on using my available personality to upgrade my formed personality. Holding this principle foremost in my thoughts gives me fresh hope and motivation, whereas without such a thought, I felt the full weight of all my past bad choices. Of course many consequences of errors and poor judgment linger in the present, yet I've lightened the load I carry and have rebalanced what remains. At the same time, I am continually increasing my awareness of and ability to transform daily existence and reclaim some small part of what might have been my original personality.

Equally important is clarity on what meaning is, where it comes from, and the role it plays in daily life. No longer do I search for meaning, as if it were to be found in some activity outside myself, as in longing to replace a meaningless job with something I might consider worthwhile in the eyes of the world. Though I cringe now, it seems that much of my earlier seeking for this false sense of meaning was little more than a desire to feel important, an inept attempt at validating my own worth.

When I sought meaning and purpose in the external, I starved my own life. My choices were always constricted by what would achieve an end result and win approval, regardless of the cost to my health or my psychological well-being. The workaholic label pinned on me was bad enough. Far worse was the realization, appearing only when I sporadically raised my head from my work, that I did not feel sincere about the work that I was sacrificing everything for.

I now understand that meaning is not "out there." It is a subjective psychological experience, and I myself can choose activities from anywhere on the palette of life as opportunities for making meaning. They become meaningful not in and of themselves, but as I consciously link the opportunity to the value that I honor.

2. *What I accomplished:* I have reevaluated the functions of all my rituals and daily habits and have become consistent in practice. Whereas before I'd thought of them mainly as sideline activities, even self-indulgences in some cases — "real life" was success in the eyes of the outer world — I now see them as primary meaning opportunities. These morning and evening rituals that support good habits, and help weed out the bad, help me live at a higher, healthier level and thus give rise to the ability to name my own life purpose.

As I returned to the first week's work to review my original menu of meaning opportunities, items that had seemed strange and even extraneous to me at the time, I see that ten of the original fifteen are in regular practice and fully integrated into my life. The remaining five are in progress, and I have my eye out for more. I find it interesting that I have not looked at the original list since the second lesson, when I created my meaning opportunity mix, yet every menu item has remained active in my thoughts, and I have accomplished most with pleasure and ease.

3. How it helped me: I am now far less stressed about the tumult of accidents and obstacles and delays and irritations of daily life. None of these really blocks access to meaning, as I once believed; thus, I no longer demand that outer life behave in any particular way. I am tolerant of aberrations, because my meaning-making opportunities are independent of such events. Once I might have interpreted some upset as a "sign" portending good or bad for whatever work I had in progress — I did this, even though I am not superstitious.

No more. Though I am aware of vast oceans of forces beyond my or anyone else's control, I still know that I am in charge of choices I make within the current that carries me. As I continue to choose what I value, I can organize my days around opportunities to activate those values.

With this new assurance, I have willingly undertaken a new work assignment that lies outside my old comfort zone. I am supported by a new constancy in the rituals that support my effort by allowing me to acknowledge what feels troubling, and then to nourish fresh positive thoughts based on clearer sight. Though a recovering workaholic, I trust the skills I've been developing through the boot camp drill not only to keep me fit but also to continue the upgrade of my personality.

4. What I would like to focus on going forward: Exploration. I want to experiment with new avenues of publishing and explore multimedia in greater depth. I also want to take advantage of wider networking opportunities and possible partnerships just now appearing on the horizon.

Yet, as always, a big issue affecting any such steps is a lifelong shyness, which I continually work to overcome. I've come to realize that, despite whatever legacy of shyness comes from my past, in the present it is a day-to-day choice either to be shy or to be more open and outgoing. And so I arrive back where I began: with the need to upgrade my personality.

Joanne: Practice, Practice, Practice

Joanne from Montreal, contemplating starting her first Internet business, completed the prompts this way:

1. What I learned: I have gained so much clarity about the obstacles that have stood in the way of my making value-based meaning efforts in my life, and obstacles that challenge me still. Really, it's startling to see how old religious beliefs and influences from my care providers have affected my ability to make efforts on my own life purposes, even to the point of being able to think for myself and recognize the truth about my life. Accepting responsibility for this state of being and level of consciousness is liberating in that I realize how free I am now to think, act, and grow according to my preferences. It is challenging too, in that in some ways I am just like a child in my skills and abilities to live a self-determined life. This will take more learning, support, and practice, practice, practice.

2. What I accomplished: I have really internalized the knowledge that making time to think critically and then taking relevant action, the next right step, is the antidote to passivity in my life. Using the strategies and tools of boot camp, doing the work of really thinking and writing about my life purposes, has given me the basic structural framework on which I can build my life from here on out.

I am using most of the resources offered in boot camp daily, such as doing meaning-making check-ins; staying alert to self-sabotage and distractions from others; using the journal to stay honest about my thoughts, feelings, self-talk, and self-deceptions; using affirmations; and using my icon and life purpose statement. Really committing to using these resources, especially the teachings about upgrading my personality, and making them an indispensable part of my daily life, is my stellar accomplishment.

3. How it helped me: I am re-creating my identity as a woman equal to living my own life, making my own values-based meaning, and accurately assessing my circumstances and acting on them, instead of just changing my attitude toward them or compromising myself right out of existence. I now challenge the formed-personality utterances of my family members and friends, especially when what they are saying relates to me. I speak up for myself and enforce my boundaries when I must, and I am not afraid to disagree with others or meet with disapproval. I realize that everyone has their admirers and their detractors, and so do I. I can live with that.

4. What I would like to focus on going forward: I will focus on all the years of living I have before me. I will take action on my life purposes every day, so that my future life can be closer to what I imagine and desire for myself. I will continue to implement the steps and strategies of boot camp until they become my habitual way of thinking, responding, and acting in my life. I want to take it from here and become a skilled values-based meaning-maker.

Julie: Meeting a Bar Set High

Julie, a fabric artist from West Virginia, shared her final report:

My biggest takeaway from boot camp is this: it truly is up to me to create the life I want through the practice of creating meaning. Coming into this boot camp I knew that, yet I especially love when others articulate ideas you feel to be true. When others share your knowing, it empowers you. Regarding life's purpose, I agree that we shouldn't wait till someone else hands them to us. However, this notion doesn't mutually exclude having faith in a Supreme Being, either. We can be guided by our belief in God, but it's still up to each of us to create meaning and find our purpose with what we're given. God is not a puppeteer.

During much of my earlier life I suffered the creative's curse, a severe case of the existential blues, expecting outside forces to create meaning for me, to show me what my life was supposed to be for. In the past several years, it's been ever clearer to me that I am creator of my world, and this boot camp drives home the point that creating meaning takes effort. That was the hard part of all this; *boot camp* is an appropriate term! Do I sometimes tire of life's little necessities? Yes! For example, I love to cook but would love even more to hire a cook so I can spend more time in my meaning zone. Yet — and this is a big yet — the Zen Buddhists say, "Before enlightenment, chop wood, carry water. After enlightenment, chop wood, carry water." Regardless of where you are in your spiritual life, you still have to take care of the necessities.

So part of my task involves learning to also create meaning in the necessities rather than viewing them as tedious chores. I'm discovering different ways of being while doing, different attitudes about the necessities. Doing so has brought me full circle to my values. Because I value life, shouldn't I value everything that sustains my life? I value good food because it nourishes my body. If I lovingly prepare my food, seeing it not as a must-do to survive but instead as a way to care for myself, it will benefit my body even more than if I prepare that food because I have to. Living is itself meaningful. If we could accept the miracle that we are, maybe we'd view life's necessities with a larger heart.

My challenge isn't discovering my purpose; I already have a clear vision of that. My challenges are letting go of needing to control life's details; letting go of outcomes and letting noncritical chores go unfinished or accepting that my helpers will do them differently; and finding the courage to do what's required of me to pursue my multiple visions so that I can fulfill my purpose. This latter challenge carries with it a need for stronger faith in my visions and less worry about whether they are doable. They *are* doable, just very grand. It doesn't help that I set a high bar! But rather than lower that bar, I would like to raise my faith, courage, and motivation to meet it.

As to the four prompts:

1. What I learned: Creating meaning takes effort. Sometimes I feel like expending it, and sometimes I don't. But I know that either way, the choice is mine and the amount of effort I put into it will determine how much, how deeply, and how often I experience meaning.

2. What I accomplished: I have a solid frame for creating more meaning, a system I can turn to when I feel beat up by life. I created a mantra, a touchstone (my symbol), and a list (my menu) of meaningful things, which I will use to guide my creation process.

3. How it helped me: This boot camp confirmed my belief that I am the creator of my world. It gave me tools to dig deeper and got me thinking about different ways to balance my life for maximum enjoyment. In creating my menu, I also got to see just how many different things I love, what's truly important to me, and that as I grow and change, so will the ranking I give to different menu items.

4. What I would like to focus on going forward: Finding more joy in life's necessities rather than perceiving some as nagging obstacles to meaning creation. Also, I want to incorporate more activities from my meaning menu into my day and use my meaning activities more effectively to feed my life's purpose.

Annette: Right Here, Right Now

Annette, a writer from Savannah, completed the four prompts this way:

1. What I learned: I learned to pay attention to and take charge of my thoughts, especially the old, old ones that tell me I am inadequate, incapable, lazy, and so on. I have plenty of evidence to the contrary — but even if I didn't, those thoughts don't serve me. Besides, they're stale and boring.

I've learned to stay away from folks who weigh me down when I'm trying to keep moving. I can love them and, until I can let their words simply fall on the floor between us, take what I want and let the rest go, I can stay away from them. This may mean ending some relationships altogether.

I know to seize the day. Every day is an opportunity to make some meaning, however small, and take some steps, however tiny, toward my values and my meaning. Seize the hour. Seize the moment.

I must acknowledge the meaning I'm making. This is critical. Part of my life purpose statement is to make a contribution. I bring a big bag of apples and a large loaf of sourdough home from the soup kitchen in good conscience because I give half to my next-door neighbor, the grad student who lives even closer to the edge than I do. Now I recognize that as simple generosity and also as contributing meaning to my life.

I enjoy knitting and do it a lot, partly because it helps me stay calm. Friends who can afford to buy nice wool yarns give me their leftovers, and I knit them into hats and blankets for homeless adults and kids. Yes, it's good for me; but in addition, it contributes meaning to my life and perhaps to my friends' lives as well.

Another part of my life purpose statement is to take care of myself. Noticing unhelpful thoughts and disputing them contributes to my experience of meaning. Acknowledging uncomfortable feelings and not running away from them or denying them contributes to my experience of meaning. Breaking an old habit and consulting a doctor rather than ignoring a trouble-some symptom also surprisingly contributes to my experience of meaning. And when I arrange for my books to be formatted so I can epublish them, I contribute meaning to my life; and I hope they're also a contribution to others' lives.

I learned to make, not wait for, meaning. To define what meaning is for me and to find ways to make it and notice it. To find meaning in aspects of my life that right now seem meaningless, because that alone will create lots of meaning investments.

Finally, I learned how important it is to be intentional. To determine what kinds of meaning I need in my life every day, and also what I look for less frequently. To then decide each day what my meaning investments will be, what periods of time will be meaning neutral, and how I can minimize meaning drains.

2. *What I accomplished:* I clarified what is important to me, what I need to change about myself to live the way I want, how the parts of my life fit together, and what gives me joy. Then I created a nine-word statement of purpose that holds that meaning for me, and posted it where I can see it every day.

I also chose a sigil (a symbol used in magic) that visually represents my life purpose and the mystery of it and created a mantra that is breathtaking in its impact when I say it to myself. So breathtaking, in fact, that I have to be intentional about saying it, or I'll completely forget it. I have it written down in many places where I'll see it every day.

I plugged into a powerful source of energy by understand-ing that I can observe my thoughts, choose which help me and which don't, decide what I think is true about what I say to myself, and change what I need. In other words, I don't have to believe everything I think. Likewise, I don't have to act on everything I feel.

On a practical level, I listed a daily baby step toward accomplishing the meaning I most want to make: self-publishing the many books that I've written. It's also what scares me the most, so each day is a teeny-tiny step, titles for the books, learning about formatting, and so on. Each of these steps feels like climbing a mountain, so I celebrate them by writing them down on my calendar and telling my creativity coconspirator, an artist friend, that I got them accomplished.

3. How boot camp helped me: The metaphor of boot camp in itself helps me a lot. Complete change, constant testing, starting the day with attention and living it with intention, quick thinking, pride, and even enjoyment in repetitive tasks: all that makes a lot of sense to me.

Another boot camp element has proven particularly helpful: the idea that I can tap into my reserves and that I *have* emotional, physical, mental, and spiritual reserves. This is especially important to me now, when my life is at a low ebb and has been for some time. Financially, emotionally, physically, and mentally I'm struggling. But I can step up enough to make a phone call to my creativity partner, commit to writing five hundred words, and report that I've done it.

I can get myself to leave home at least a few days a week to connect with other people and do something to contribute to my community. I can speak from my experience, strength, and hope at meetings, and perhaps something I say will benefit someone. I can swallow my pride, go to the soup kitchen, enjoy talking with folks there, and bring back food to help my neighbor and myself.

These are all things I can do within my present circumstances, because as you've said throughout boot camp, I have
to live my life purpose right here and right now. In one sense,
right here and right now is not ideal; in another sense, it's perfect, because it's here, where I am, and now, which is all any
of us has to work with. Right here and right now is reality, not
escaping from it into fantasy or addiction or torpor, or wallow-
ing in self-pity or indecision. My life is pretty danged good when
I let it be.

Finally — not the end of what has helped me, but the end
of what I can write about at this point in the process — you
talk a lot about courage and persistence, stepping up to life,
and confronting life circumstances and not letting them stop
us. You encourage me to be a warrior on my own behalf. But
you also teach me that every minute is a new opportunity to
step up, to pick myself up when necessary, to choose again, to
reorient myself to my life meaning, and to insist that my life has
meaning and to claim it. So, yes, it's an all-or-nothing decision;
and no, it's not all or nothing in the living of it.

4. What I will focus on going forward: I'll keep taking little steps
toward getting my books published, and I'll record and celebrate them. I'll write the short nonfiction pieces and find a good
use for them. I'll pay attention to my thoughts and feelings,
confronting those that make progress feel like wading through
cold water; and, if necessary, I'll wade through cold water
sometimes. I'll embrace the huge benefit of having a creativity
coconspirator and let myself ask for and accept help as well as
offer and give help.

I'll take care of myself in the ways I know I have to, because
this life requires training, just as a warrior's does. The training

may not be long nighttime marches in full gear, but it's just as exacting and essential. If I think of it as training, I'm less likely to whine. And I'll let my life be pretty danged good as much as possible.

The goal of all this is to live the mystery of meaning and especially of creativity, and add my voice to the heart songs of others. As Popeye said, I yam what I yam; and I see and experience and know what I know, and I speak as I do. That's not nothing, even if, maybe especially if, it's not an ultimate something.

You may find that it serves you to write your own life purpose boot camp final report. Organize your report as I've indicated above, or any way you like.

Existential Maturity

Phil Jackson, the famous basketball coach, was fond of remarking that while people never change, they do mature. That's an interesting distinction, isn't it? Apparently you must remain you, but you can become a mature version of you. I think we've been talking about something similar throughout this book: that you can grow into a mature understanding of meaning and life purpose and as a result become an existentially adult version of yourself.

Having life purposes makes no one a saint. But deciding on your life purposes and trying to live them are signs of maturity. Living our life purposes on an angry day, when it would be so easy to lash out, may help us do the right thing instead of the wrong thing. Remembering on a bleak day that the experience of meaning can and will return helps us to opt for hope rather than despair. Living our life purposes may help us love a little more than is actually in our heart to love and hate a little less than is actually in our heart to hate. Our life purposes are reminders that we've made decisions, that we have options, that we can get a grip, and that we can make ourselves proud.

We've seen in the reports of life purpose boot campers just how tumultuous, intricate, contradictory, and irregular life can be. Who doesn't have shadows to deal with? Who isn't embroiled in the reality of circumstances? Who isn't unequal to the idea of "life as project"? Yet every participant in my online boot camp wanted to try and knew why it was important to do so. Like them, you know what you have in you: both a taste for carelessness and a taste for heroism.

This is a book for human beings as they are, for creatures who have evolved exactly as we have evolved, who are pushed and pulled in exactly the ways that we are pushed and pulled, who would like to do better and who would like to do more and who would also like to do nothing and who would also like to get even. I am not a futurist, I have no crystal ball, and I have no clue whatsoever where our species may go. But I do know where we are. Don't you?

I'm selling the idea of value-based meaning-making as a useful, even elegant approximate answer to the central question with which life presents us: Why do this and not that? Why wake up and stretch and get on with life and not turn over and pout? Why speak truth to power and not just pad our bank account? Why hug our child rather than berating and belittling him? Why sing, why dance, why stay sober, why foment a revolution? Why anything? The central answer is that we can conceive of a life, our life, resting firmly on the pillars of the life purposes that we ourselves name and live.

The central mechanism for living is making value-based meaning. Then you can answer each and every "why" question, from the most trivial to the most momentous, by saying to the world and by saying to yourself: "I have my life purposes, I've named them for myself and I understand them pretty darn well, and I will choose in light of them." This way of answering helps prevent you from answering from those other places that also reside within you: the place that doesn't care, the place that has no energy, the place of anxiety and fear, the place just marking time, the place of custom and conformity, the place that's concluded that life is a cheat.

Your life purpose work, from which flow your life purpose statement, your life purpose icon, your life purpose mantra, and your complete life purpose vision, may save you. It may save you from losing years to habit and to carelessness. It may save you from hiding out or giving yourself away. It may save you from your own doubts, your own fears, and your own resistance. It may save you from yourself. To employ a last military analogy: your life purposes armor you. They protect you from distractions, from infatuations, and from returning to a life of doubting and seeking.

Barbarity, generosity, and everything human will exist until we are some other kind of creature. Everything that makes us human and that affects us as humans will continue. Waves will continue to crash against us, threatening to throw us off course. Life is like that. Right here, right now, you get to decide who you will attempt to be. If you've read this book but not actually lived it, it is time to start again from the beginning and really live it this time. This boot camp requires your attention and engagement, and I hope you will bring both those things to the task.

Remember Sisyphus, a king in Greek mythology and the subject of Albert Camus's essay "The Myth of Sisyphus"? Sisyphus is condemned by the gods to forever roll a rock to the top of a mountain, whereupon the rock rolls back down again. Camus allows that Sisyphus — that any human being — can still experience freedom, meaning, and happiness even in dreadful circumstances like those. I wonder if that is literally true. I wonder if dreadful circumstances can't defeat even the most steadfast existentialist. But few of us are quite as condemned as Sisyphus. We have more freedom than he did — and we must use it. Nothing in the universe will condemn us for not making use of our available freedom — nothing, that is, except our own conscience.

About the Author

Dr. Eric Maisel is the author of more than forty works of fiction and nonfiction. Widely regarded as America's foremost creativity coach, he founded the profession of creativity coaching and provides core trainings for the Creativity Coaching Association. As a California-licensed family therapist, Dr. Maisel is part of the critical psychiatry movement investigating alternatives to the current mental health system. His interests in meaning and life purpose have prompted him to develop natural psychology, a new psychology of meaning.

He writes the "Rethinking Psychology" column for *Psychology Today*, blogs for Mad in America and the Global

Summit on Diagnostic Alternatives, contributes pieces on mental health to the *Huffington Post*, and leads life purpose boot camp classes and trains life purpose boot camp instructors. He presents at workshop centers such as Omega, Kripalu, Esalen, and Rowe; at events such as the Paris Writers Workshop; at annual conferences of organizations such as Romance Writers of America and the American Psychological Association; and in locations such as San Francisco, New York, London, Paris, Prague, Rome, and Berlin.

Dr. Maisel lives in the San Francisco Bay Area, where he maintains an active creativity coaching practice. He can be reached at ericmaisel@hotmail.com, and you can learn more about his books, workshops, trainings, and services at www.ericmaisel.com.